D1191880

The European
Common Mark

The European Common Market

GROWTH AND PATTERNS OF TRADE AND PRODUCTION

Ingo Walter

FREDERICK A. PRAEGER, Publishers
New York · Washington · London

The purpose of the Praeger Special Studies is to make specialized research monographs in U.S. and international economics and politics available to the academic, business, and government communities. For further information, write to the Special Projects Division, Frederick A. Praeger, Publishers, 111 Fourth Avenue, New York, N.Y. 10003.

FREDERICK A. PRAEGER, PUBLISHERS
111 Fourth Avenue, New York, N.Y. 10003, U.S.A.
5 Cromwell Place, London S.W. 7, England

Published in the United States of America in 1967
by Frederick A. Praeger, Inc., Publishers

Second printing, 1968

Library of Congress Catalog Card Number: 66-26576

Printed in the United States of America

PREFACE

The question arises, from time to time, how successful the European Common Market has really been in directly or indirectly benefiting the national economies of the six member countries. Efforts have been made to arrive at a meaningful estimate of the impact of the EEC, but most have ended in speculation. The reasons for this are twofold: First, the period of existence of the EEC, historically speaking, has been relatively short and it has therefore been difficult to discuss fundamental changes in trade patterns, economic structure, or rate of economic growth of the community. Second, shifts in the structure of the national economies, as well as changes in the direction and volume of trade flows and the rate of over-all economic growth, are influenced by a great many other factors which are not necessarily associated with economic integration. Hence it is difficult to isolate the effect of the Common Market upon these variables in any really meaningful way.

The purpose of this study is to attempt to determine--or, at least, suggest--the impact of economic integration in the EEC on a single aspect of the economic life of the member states: the volume and direction of intra-community trade. This is done for the longest period of time for which the necessary data were complete and readily available.

The study begins by presenting the theory justifying all attempts at regional economic integration and applying this theoretical foundation to the institutional environment which characterizes the European Economic Community. Thereafter, the *de facto* liberalization of internal barriers to trade is presented along with an attempt to determine the response to these developments in the form of changes in the volume and direction of trade, both in the aggregate and via a commodity breakdown of total trade. Finally, an effort is made to ascertain whether the changes in trade patterns and growth were associated with a shift in the geographical locus of production within the Common Market.

At each stage, the observed developments are related to the pertinent aspects of the theory of economic integration. Hence it is possible to roughly determine whether or not, and how closely, the facts substantiate or refute the theoretical indications. At the same time, however, it must be recognized that the results obtained are subject to a great many limitations, due primarily to the complexity of the subject and to the multiplicity of factors involved. In order to minimize the danger of drawing conclusions from insufficient or misleading information, a variety of approaches are used in the case of each individual analysis.

The data used cover the 1958-63 period and, where possible, the years 1958-65. Generally, comparisons are drawn between comparable periods of time before and after the EEC was formed. Hence the currency of the data is not of determining importance for purposes of gauging the direction and general magnitude of the impact of the EEC on trade volumes and patterns.

While this study can contain no precise estimate of the effect of the EEC on trade and production patterns, it does suggest the direction of change as well as its general order of magnitude. Perhaps of equal or greater interest is the exposition of the evident limitations and difficulties besetting all studies of this kind.

The bulk of the work connected with this study was undertaken at the Graduate School of Business Administration, New York University, which provided an environment conducive to serious thought and discussion. Thanks are due Professors Holger L. Engberg, Solomon Fabricant, John Fayerweather, Robert G. Hawkins, and John E. Kramer, Jr., who read all or parts of the study and offered numerous suggestions and criticisms. Only some of these are incorporated here, so that the author must fully bear the responsibility for any remaining faults in the analysis and omission of pertinent material. Miss Jan Finke and Mrs. Jan Munro capably handled the retyping chores, with my wife patiently suffering through the entire first draft of the manuscript. The author is also indebted to the J.B. Lippincott Company for permission to reprint excerpts from The Common Market: Economic Integration in Europe, published in 1965, in Chapter 2 of the present study. Finally, for financial support during the various phases of researching and writing the author is indebted to the Ford Foundation through its Workshop program at New York University, and to the Committee on Research at the University of Missouri at St. Louis.

Ingo Walter

St. Louis, Missouri

CONTENTS

LIST OF TABLES

Tables in Appendix

The European Common Market

CHAPTER 1 INTRODUCTION

Much has been written about the impact of international economic integration upon the national economies of the participating states. Generally, integration is thought to be highly beneficial for two sets of reasons. First, it is said to bring about a change in supply and demand patterns in such a way as to maximize consumer welfare and minimize economic costs of supply within the free-trade area: the so-called static effects of integration. Second, it is said to confer upon the member states some of the advantages enjoyed by large nations: free mobility of factors of production, economies of scale, increased feasibility of innovation, and so forth. These are called the "dynamic" effects of integration. The major part of this study is concerned with the <u>static</u> effects, and attempts to determine the degree to which the changes in trade and production patterns predicted by the theory of economic integration actually materialized in one integration project: the European Common Market.

The theoretical arguments in favor of economic union are highly persuasive and, assuming that a variety of political barriers can be overcome, hold great promise for the participating nations of any successful economic union. Thus the past decade has seen a rash of integration projects both among developed and underdeveloped nations. Besides the European Economic Community (EEC), the Latin American Free Trade Association (LAFTA), European Free Trade Association (EFTA), Central American Common Market (CACM), and the Council for Mutual Economic Assistance (COMECON) are prominent examples. These are in addition to the highly successful Belgium-Luxembourg Economic Union (BLEU), incorporated after World War II in the Benelux economic union. All of these integration projects are based on the idea that the theoretical foundation is fundamentally sound and that benefits derived from integration will more than offset the political and economic adjustments which must be made. A major purpose of this study is to try to determine whether this belief is justified by analyzing the impact of the most advanced major integration project--the EEC--upon economic relations among the member states; or, at least, in the course of this attempt to indicate the kinds of problems involved in justifying or denying this belief.

Changes in trade and production patterns within the Common Market would appear to be the best indication of the actual shifts in the economic structure of the EEC resulting from integration. The reallocation of production from high-cost to low-cost community producers changes the geographical locus of production and at the same time increases the volume of intra-EEC trade. Similarly, the broadened range of consumer or user choice which results from integration likewise increases the volume of intra-area trade; whether this consumption effect also tends to result in a shift in the geographical locus of production, however, is not clear. At the same time, community tariff discrimination with respect to non-member countries would be expected to stimulate the volume of internal trade at the expense of trade with the rest of the world.

The primary questions which this study attempts to answer, then, are these: Did the formation of the EEC have a significant impact on the growth and direction of intra-area trade during the period covered? If so, were the changes which occurred in accordance with those anticipated by the theory of economic integration? Which aspects of the theory seem to carry the most weight, and which seem to be of little importance? Finally, what happened to the geographical locus of production, and how much of the growth of intra-EEC trade can be accounted for by production shifts?

Needless to say, the questions under examination here are highly complex and the number of variables involved is large. Hence the limitations to the validity of any conclusions drawn from the analysis will doubtlessly be of considerable importance. Nevertheless, the problem is still worth study, both as an empirical test of the validity of the theory and as an indication of what the future may hold for other, less advanced attempts at economic integration.

There has been surprisingly little extensive empirical work published on this subject. Despite the voluminous literature on the theoretical implications of economic integration, there have been relatively few extensive tests of the theory, both because of the comparatively short period of time the community has been in existence and the fact that the economic impact of the EEC is inexorably intertwined with a large number of other economic, political, and social factors. There is little doubt, however, that the number of factual examinations of Common Market trade patterns will grow as the community develops in future years.[1]

While the empirical literature on the effects of customs unions on internal trade growth and patterns is sparse in the case of the EEC, there are studies available on other attempts at economic integration, notably the European Free Trade Association and the Benelux economic union.[2] Only a small part of the methodology used in these studies is transferable to the present case, however, due to greatly differing institutional arrangements and the varying nature of the economies involved in the respective integration projects. Moreover, the conclusions reached in some of these studies are not entirely convincing by themselves since they, too, attempt to isolate a single variable in a highly complex phenomenon.

Hopefully, the present study will add to the stock of knowledge already available about the economic impact of integration upon the member countries. At the same time, it may serve as a guide to further research into a problem which promises to be of substantial importance in international economic relations for some time to come, whatever the immediate fate of the EEC.

Notes to Chapter 1

1. For examples of research done in this area see: P.J. Verdoorn and F.J.M. Meyer zu Schlochten, "Trade Diversion and Trade Creation in the Common Market," Intégration Européenne et Réalité Economique (Paris: OECD, 1964), pp. 95-138, and reprinted in Central Planning Bureau Reprint Series, No. 93 (The Hague, 1965).

Alexander Lamfalussy, The United Kingdom and the Six (Homewood, Ill.: Richard D. Irwin, 1963).

2. James E. Meade et al., Case Studies in European Economic Union (London: Oxford University Press, 1962).

James E. Meade, The Belgium-Luxembourg Economic Union (Princeton: International Finance Section, Department of Economics, Princeton University, 1956).

European Free Trade Association, EFTA Trade (New York: McGraw-Hill, 1965, 1966).

CHAPTER 2 FORMAL PROVISIONS ON TRADE AND TARIFFS

Before an analysis of the changes in EEC trade and production patterns in response to the formation of the Common Market is undertaken, a short statement of the formal trade provisions of the Rome Treaty may help place these developments in perspective.[1]

At present, the European Common Market is composed of the six signatory nations of the Rome Treaty of 1957: Belgium, France, Germany, Italy, Luxembourg, and the Netherlands. A somewhat more limited form of economic integration than that contemplated in the EEC is gradually to be extended to the overseas territorial possessions of the member countries over a prolonged period of time in the form of a modified free-trade area. Former territories which have gained independence may be associated with the EEC in a similar manner if they wish to participate. Non-member European nations likewise are not excluded by the Rome Treaty from full or associate membership.[2] If such countries prove themselves willing to accept all obligations which accompany membership, on an equal footing with the original six, they may be admitted to full partnership contingent, however, upon full and unanimous consent of the existing members.

Moreover, the EEC is empowered to reach agreements and association with other international organizations and economic or political groupings.[3] The OECD, the IMF, and the Latin American Free Trade Association (LAFTA) are examples in this category.

All countries, either individually or through existing international organizations, could in principle become associated with the EEC. Such association could come about in various ways, but full or associate membership in the community and bilateral trade agreements with the EEC seem most likely. The practicability or desirability of an ambitious extension of the EEC itself is still very much a topic of debate and conjecture.[4]

The Rome Treaty presents a concise summary of the basic aims of the Common Market.[5] The primary underlying thought is the creation of a regional, integrated economic complex which will help ensure the generally accepted economic policy goals of full employment, price level stability, rapid growth, and viable external balance. The economies of the individual partner countries are gradually to adjust to the changes brought about by integration and ultimately form a homogeneous union. A basic premise underlying the Common Market economic philosophy as expressed in the Treaty is the idea that integration will lead to an efficient utilization of productive capacity within the community. This, in turn, can only be achieved by means of the optimal utilization of the agents involved in the production-distribution cycle--labor, capital, land, technology, and entrepreneurship--and unhindered movement of goods throughout the integrated area.

Chapter 4 outlines the primary impediments to trade among the EEC countries prior to 1958. In addition to quotas and tariffs, they included a variety of fees, licenses, specific regulations, and other impediments. Competition among countries was widely distorted and at times eliminated. In addition, differences prevailing in national taxation systems, freight rate structures, anti-cartel legislation, and social insurance laws contributed additional divergences to the cost-price structures of individual national industries and economies. Government manipulation of exchange rates and exchange rationing, imposed primarily for balance of payments reasons during the postwar years, further complicated matters. Finally, hindrances to the free flow of direct and portfolio investment capital across national frontiers, as well as the restriction of labor mobility, impeded the effective allocation of these two productive factors.

INTERNAL TARIFF PROVISIONS

It is these impediments to the efficient working of the European regional economy that the Treaty of Rome purports to eliminate. Five main stipulations cover the essential economic provisions of the agreement. First, the free flow of goods and services is assured between the several member nations by eliminating all restrictions to intra-EEC trade.[6] A uniform external tariff is envisaged between the EEC and third countries with the community acting as a unit in trade negotiations with non-member countries. Second, the coordination and harmonization of the various national transportation systems is to be effected as rapidly as possible in order to eliminate the distortions induced by differing freight rates and other transport costs.[7] Third, the economic policies of the participating nations are to be coordinated in order to facilitate the achievement of high levels of employment, price level stability, and viable external balance throughout the community.[8] Fourth, the legal conditions under which competition takes place between firms are to be harmonized in order to impede monopoly and cartel organization unless it is thought to contribute in some way to the economic welfare of the EEC as a whole.[9] Finally, the unrestricted mobility of labor, capital, technology, and entrepreneurship between the member states is to be assured.[10]

Full integration of the economies of the member countries into one unified regional economic grouping is to be achieved primarily through implementation of these five basic measures. The part of the EEC program of action which initially is perhaps of primary importance, and the one with which we will mainly be concerned here, is the elimination of internal trade barriers and the formation of a common external tariff wall.

An important driving force behind the tariff provisions of the Rome Treaty, and a large factor in the significant successes achieved in their implementation during the first six years of the EEC, has been the idea of a "timetable." It was anticipated by the authors of the Treaty, that no matter how agreeable the individual tariff negotiators would be in principle regarding the general objective of reductions in intra-Community customs duties, there would always be instances where negotiators would plead for "a little more time." This related especially to possible adverse economic effects of tariff reductions on specific segments of the member's respective national economies and the ensuing possibility of political repercussions. The idea of a timetable, however, laid down in advance and agreed upon by all participating countries, proved to be a powerful means of preventing the negotiators from stalling. It was generally agreed that procrastination on the part of a single country would hold up or disrupt the tariff reduction process, thereby delaying the entire advance of the economic integration in the community.

The original timetable set down by the Treaty of Rome in 1957 provided for a "transition period" of twelve years, which could be shortened or prolonged, but not extended beyond fifteen years. This made the deadline for full EEC economic integration December 31, 1969, with the possibility of extension until the end of 1972. The transition period was divided into three "stages" of four years each. Tariff reductions were designed to be effected in a series of 10 per cent steps at specified dates throughout the transition period, and minimum goals were set to be achieved by the end of each stage.

During the first four-year stage of the transition period all EEC decisions, except for those involving tariff and quota reductions, were formulated on the basis of unanimity. According to the Rome Treaty, December 31, 1961, was designated as the date for a vote to determine whether or not to proceed into the second stage of the transition period. If unanimity could not be achieved, the first stage might be prolonged for one or two years, thus slowing the process of integration and giving the individual countries more time to make the necessary adjustments. If a unanimous decision to pass from the first to the second stage could not be reached by the end of the second additional year, a qualified majority vote would then suffice to cancel the impeding vetoes and clear the way for passage to the second stage.

All during the second stage, the qualified majority rule was intended to apply to all EEC decisions, and the passage from the second to the third stage of the transition period was to be automatic. Only the unanimous vote of all members might prolong the second stage, as intended by the Rome Treaty. Thus, after the end of the first stage unanimous agreement was needed to postpone integration, rather than to perpetuate it. The same procedure held for the ultimate ending of the transition period.

Historically, the transition from the first to the second stage was accomplished during a marathon negotiating session in January of 1962. The device of "stopping the clock" was employed in order to enable the delegates to continue negotiations until final agreement could be reached on January 14, 1962. Officially, the EEC entered the second stage of economic integration on January 1, 1962, exactly four years after the Treaty of Rome came into force. The first great hurdle to the achievement of full integration was thus overcome and a great deal of uncertainty was removed, since the unanimity rule concerning further integration steps was no longer in force. In a sense, the EEC was thought to have passed the point of no return. The only thing which could still postpone achievement of a full economic union by December 31, 1969, was the unanimous decision of the member countries at the end of 1965 to prolong the transition period.

The Rome Treaty originally stipulated that, by the end of the first stage (January 1, 1962) internal tariffs were to be reduced to 70 per cent of the levels in force on January 1, 1957. At the end of the second stage, customs duties on intra-community trade were to be lowered to 40 per cent of the 1957 levels. According to the prevailing economic conditions, the EEC Council of Ministers would fix the elimination of the remaining tariffs at the end of the second stage. In any event, by December 31, 1969, all tariffs and quotas on internal trade were to have been eliminated. However, subsequent events have served to considerably accelerate this original timetable.

In addition to the idea of a timetable, a second principle completes the highly effective Common Market tariff-reduction program. The "across the board," or "linear," principle dictates that tariffs be reduced not commodity by commodity, as, for example, was the case in past GATT negotiations, but rather on all goods at once. In addition, tariff reductions are undertaken in each case by a set percentage of the level in force at the time of the signing of the Treaty of Rome. In this way the elimination of internal trade barriers is virtually taken out of the hands of the negotiators and, by being formulated in an <u>ex ante</u> fashion, the EEC tariff reduction program embodies a considerable degree of automaticity. Certain products, such as agricultural commodities, where the impact of categorical tariff reductions upon national industries or economies could prove severe, were exempted from the timetable and governed by special regulations.[11] For example, all intra-EEC agricultural quotas, duties, and minimum prices have been replaced by a system of variable levies.

The actual elimination of internal tariffs on manufactured goods began with a 10 per cent reduction, applied on January 1, 1959, one year after the Treaty of Rome took effect. Two additional reductions of 10 per cent each were planned at intervals of eighteen months. This would have brought the internal tariff levels at the end of the first stage of the transition period, as stated earlier, to 70 per cent of their 1957 levels. Originally, the second stage was to include two 10 per cent reductions at eighteen-month intervals and one at the conclusion of that period, thus bringing tariffs down to the 40 per cent level on January 1, 1966.[12]

By the end of 1959, however, it had become evident that the adjustment difficulties which accompany tariff removal were proving to be considerably less severe than originally anticipated. The willingness and ability of industry to adapt to the new conditions exceeded expectations. Consequently, it was decided on May 12, 1960, to accelerate the pace of integration in line with the high degree of adaptability demonstrated by business and industry, and by January 1, 1962, customs duties on industrial goods had already been reduced to 60 per cent of the 1957 levels, which more than fulfilled the Treaty's requirements of a minimum 30 per cent cut in the basic tariff during the first stage. Two further cuts of 10 per cent during the marathon negotiations on January 7, 1962, and in July, 1963, brought the intra-community customs duties down to 40 per cent of their 1957 levels at the end of 1963. In May of 1966 it was decided to eliminate all remaining internal tariffs by July 1, 1968.

It should be emphasized at this point that the Rome Treaty stipulation requiring tariff cuts of a given percentage does not necessarily mean that this reduction has to be applied to each and every product. Rather, a more flexible method was adopted whereby some discretion is allowed each individual government in applying the reductions. Whereas the first 10 per cent reduction in 1959 did indeed have to be applied uniformly, for all subsequent cuts the tariff on some goods need be lowered by as little as 5 per cent, as long as the tariff decrease as a whole amounts to the 10 per cent stipulated figure.[13] This permits the individual countries to allocate about half the burden of the reductions in order to soften the impact of domestic industries. The only basic restriction to this provision was that the tariff on each individual product had to be reduced at least 25 per cent and 50 per cent at the end of the first and second stages of the transition period, respectively.[14]

One more reduction of 10 per cent was scheduled for the remainder of the second stage: in January of 1966, thus bringing intra-EEC tariffs at the end of the second stage down to 20 per cent of their original levels. The remaining 20 per cent duty was abolished in July, 1967, thus eliminating all internal customs duties three years before the end of the planned transition period.

It was recognized from the start that the rapidity with which internal duties can be eliminated hinges mainly upon the ability of the various industrial sectors of the community to adjust to the gradual disappearance of protective trade barriers. In the event that adverse conditions should materialize at any time during the transition period, the remaining tariff reductions could in fact be postponed until 1969. The coordination of taxation systems and economic policy, which supplements and supports integration in goods and services, was planned to proceed on a schedule parallel to the removal of intra-EEC trade barriers.

Although far less important than tariffs, certain European countries traditionally levied export duties and taxes on specific products in intra-EEC trade. These were also banned in the Rome Treaty[15] and were eliminated at the end of the first stage of the transition period. Customs duties levied on certain imported consumer goods for revenue purposes were subject to the general rules for the abolition of tariffs, although the member nation retained the right to impose domestic taxes on these products as long as they remained non-discriminatory with respect to imports.

INTERNAL QUOTAS

The elimination of quantitative restrictions to internal trade progressed even more rapidly than the lowering of tariff barriers. Many European countries developed the quota system during the depression years of the 1930's. Quotas limit the importation of goods to a fixed quantum over a given time period. Like tariffs, they are usually implemented in order to protect domestic industries from foreign competition or for balance of payments reasons and, in addition, they may serve as an instrument of foreign policy. "Discriminatory" quotas contain provisions to allocate the import licenses to certain favored supplying nations. Non-discriminatory, or "global," quotas simply place a limit on the amount of a good which may be imported from all trading partners, without regard to country of origin. Reciprocal, bilateral trade agreements, longstanding political connections, or other foreign policy considerations generally are the causal forces behind selective quotas.

The Rome Treaty took explicit steps to deal with this very delicate problem. All quotas between the EEC countries, rather than remaining selective, became "global," or non-discriminatory, with respect to the exports of all member states in 1959. Each EEC country could thus participate on an equal basis with all others in exporting to another member nation under that country's quota systems. However, due to the relatively minor significance of selective quotas in trade between Common Market nations, this development had little effect on intra-EEC movement of goods. Concurrently, intra-EEC quotas were increased by 20 per cent, on the average, and by a minimum of 10 per cent in the case of any given product. Subsequent increases of 20 per cent were provided so that all quotas on intra-community trade would be eliminated by the end of the transition period at the latest. Minimum quotas were also raised annually, based upon permissible quota-imports as a percentage of domestic production.[16]

Acceleration of the pace of integration, however, permitted all quota restrictions to be abolished at the end of 1961, with the sole exception of agricultural products. In this area it was decided at that time that quotas should be "global" within the EEC and should not be less than 5.2 per cent of national output. More recently, all agricultural internal quotas have been replaced by variable levies. As will be shown later, the abolition of the remaining restrictions to internal trade, both in the form of tariffs as well as other explicit and implicit barriers to the free movement of goods and services, depends primarily upon the speed with which common economic policies can be developed.

Discrepancies between national quota systems have caused considerable difficulty in the implementation of EEC policy designed to achieve their elimination. For example, whereas one country based quotas on physical units, another employed the c.i.f. import values as a base. These difficulties were, however, successfully overcome, as evidenced by the total elimination of intra-community quotas.

Later sections of this study will show that certain special problems have developed from time to time with respect to the implementation of the provisions designed to eliminate trade barriers. For example, it has occasionally been pointed out that excessively strict interpretation of quota, licensing, and other regulations may constitute hidden restrictions on the free movement of goods across community frontiers. Presumably, the eventual harmonization of such regulations throughout the EEC and the gradual elimination of restrictive national regulatory practices will, in time, remove these hindrances of trade as well.

EXTERNAL TRADE POLICY

Although we are not directly concerned with the external trade of the EEC in this study, a discussion of the formal trade provisions of the Treaty of Rome would hardly be complete without some mention of community commercial relations with third countries. By the end of the transition period, the external trade restrictions of the EEC countries are to be equalized in the form of a common tariff wall with respect to the rest of the world. This involves the harmonization of the external tariffs maintained by the five pre-existing customs areas: Germany, France, Italy, the Netherlands, and the BLEU. At the earliest, the uniform external tariff was designed to be achieved at the end of the transition period on December 31, 1969, but no later than the end of 1972.

Common Market external tariff policy as expressed in the Rome Treaty was strongly influenced, and to some degree determined, by the General Agreement on Tariffs and Trade (GATT), of which all EEC countries are members. GATT stipulates that the external duties of a customs union must not be higher than the arithmetic average of the tariffs prevailing prior to the formation of such a union and that all trade barriers between the member nations must be eliminated within a reasonable time period. Thus, in the case of the EEC, the Rome Treaty stipulated that the Common External Tariff should have an upper limit comprising the average of the tariff levels in force on January 1, 1957, in the member countries.[17] GATT broadened the concept of customs unions so as to include customs unions-in-being, with reasonable allowance for their growth in several stages.

The Treaty of Rome clearly recognized the possibility that the categorical application of the GATT rule might conflict with the economic requirements raised by the formation of the EEC. Consequently, provisions were made for negotiations on the Common External Tariff to begin not later than the second year after the Treaty was to take effect, and to be completed before the end of the first stage of the transition period.

Maximum rates were laid down above which the external levies should under no circumstances be set: 15-25 per cent for manufactured goods, 10-15 per cent for processed raw materials and semi-finished manufactures, and 3 per cent for raw materials. As in the elimination of internal restrictions to trade, three stages were also envisaged for the implementation of the Common External Tariff. On January 1, 1962, all external tariffs within 15 per cent of the calculated arithmetic mean of the pre-EEC duties were supposed to be replaced by the common tariff.[18] In practice, however, this was accomplished on December 31, 1960. In addition, the gap between all other duties and the Common External Tariff was reduced by 30 per cent at that time.

According to the Treaty, if members encounter special difficulties in implementing the common tariff, they might postpone raising or lowering duties by authorization of the EEC Commission.[19] The number of cases where this has occurred has been limited and generally was prompted by commercial policy considerations of a temporary nature.

Originally, the second stage of the implementation of the common tariff was to take place four years later and was to consist of another 30 per cent reduction in the difference between the Common External Tariff and the pre-EEC duties. The final elimination of all external tariff differences and the actual full application of the common tariff was to occur before 1969. Actually, the second 30 per cent adjustment toward the ultimate Common External Tariff was made on July 1, 1963, instead of in 1966, as originally envisioned. The remaining adjustment of the individual national external duties to the Common External Tariff was expected to occur in line with the accelerated removal of internal trade barriers.

At the same time the institution of the Common External Tariff was contemplated, negotiations were being carried on among the EEC and the other GATT countries concerning a reduction in over-all community external tariffs, on the condition of reciprocity. The common tariff was subsequently reduced by 20 per cent in 1962 and the alignment of the national duties was pursued on this new, lower base.

For certain products, where Common Market output is considered to be insufficient to meet demand requirements, the EEC Commission is empowered to grant exemption from the common tariff. In cases where the major suppliers of a certain good have traditionally been non-member nations, duty-free or reduced tariffs may be granted to the member country concerned. Although it is clearly recognized that the unity of the Common External Tariff is impaired by such exemptions, and the formation of a true customs union is thereby endangered, a considerable number of these waivers have been granted.

Member states have also been permitted to use "tariff quotas" temporarily in order to dampen the effects of alignment. The tariff quota is distinguished from the usual quota in that it does not fix an absolute limit on the quantity of a given good which may be imported, but rather sets the amount beyond which a higher tariff rate is applied. In the EEC this might be employed in cases where a country has traditionally obtained a product from external non-member suppliers and domestic production is deemed insufficient.

With the harmonization of external tariffs, it becomes necessary for the EEC countries to coordinate their commercial relations with third countries as well. For instance, in 1962 the Council of Ministers approved an EEC Commission proposal for a common external trade policy including plans to gradually remove quantitative restrictions on trade with non-member countries, the standardization of national export and import regulations, and even the harmonization of export promotion efforts.

By the end of the transition period at the latest, the individual governments should be completely eliminated from tariff negotiations, this task being left entirely to the EEC Commission and the Council of Ministers. A pertinent example is the EEC policy in the "Kennedy-round" GATT trade negotiations. In present and future international economic organizations as well, the Common Market will be represented as one unified area.

SERVICES AND THE "RIGHT OF ESTABLISHMENT"

The Treaty of Rome guarantees that free mobility between the member countries shall not be limited to goods alone. By the end of the transition period, restrictions to the free movement and establishment of all natural and legal persons within the community are to be eliminated.[20] Any individual, legal, or natural person in the EEC may set up branches, agencies, or subsidiaries in all of the member countries without restriction of any kind. The freedom of establishment also includes the "...right to engage in and carry on non-wage-earning activities and also to set up and manage enterprises...under the conditions laid down by the law of the country or establishment for its own nationals...."[21]

No new restrictions or the right of establishment were to be introduced by any member country during the transition period. Essentially, the provisions dealing with the actual implementation of the EEC program for unhindered establishment are similar to those related to labor mobility.[22]

The Rome Treaty provides equivalent mobility with respect to services.[23] Industrial and commercial services, artisans and members of the liberal professions are to be allowed to move freely throughout the EEC, subject only to the existence of possibly contrary Treaty provisions dealing with the free movement of goods, labor, and capital. By unanimous vote of the Council of Ministers on a proposal of the Commission, citizens of non-member countries may also be granted the same privileges in this area as nationals of the six EEC countries. Insurance firms, building contractors, advertising agencies, and the motion picture industry were expected to be greatly affected by these provisions. Transportation services are also free to move within the community, although they are specifically covered under a different section of the Treaty.[24]

Steps taken to implement the provisions on free establishment of individuals and services include a detailed timetable adopted by the Council of Ministers, in consultation with the Economic and Social Committee, in December, 1961. An order of priority which is "...to ensure the freedom of establishment and the freedom to supply services..." was thus set down.[25] Those activities which were found to be especially valuable for the development of trade and production were given first priority. Measures designed to fully bring about the right of establishment and the complete liberalization of services are facilitated considerably during the second stage of the transition period, since a qualified majority vote suffices for the passage of specific measures by the Council of Ministers.

We have seen, then, how the Treaty of Rome lays out a plan of action for the creation of a unified market of the six participating countries in goods and services, and how this plan was followed during the period under consideration here. What general shifts in trade and production patterns might be expected as a result of this progression toward an economic union, based on *a priori* economic reasoning, are the subject of the following chapter.

Notes to Chapter 2

1. Trade provisions of the Rome Treaty are contained in: Interim Committee for the Common Market and EURATOM *Treaty Establishing the European Atomic Energy Community (EURATOM) and the Common Market*, and connected documents (Brussels, 1957); they are integrated in: Hans von der Groeben and H. von Boeckh, *Kommentar zum EWG - Vertrag* (Baden-Baden: August Lutzeyer, 1958).

2. Treaty of Rome, Article 237.

3. *Ibid.*, Article 238.

4. Sections of this chapter are reprinted by permission from Finn B. Jensen and Ingo Walter, *The Common Market: Economic Integration in Europe* (Philadelphia: J. B. Lippincott Company, 1965).

5. Treaty of Rome, Article 2.

6. *Ibid.*, Articles 17-37.

7. *Ibid.*, Articles 74-84.

8. *Ibid.*, Articles 92-122.

9. *Ibid.*, Articles 85-91.

10. *Ibid.*, Articles 48-73.

11. Treaty of Rome, Articles 38-40.

12. *Ibid.*, Article 14.

13. *Ibid.*

14. *Ibid.*

15. *Ibid.*, Article 16.

16. *Ibid.*, Article 33.

17. Treaty of Rome, Article 19.

18. *Ibid.*, Article 23.

19. *Ibid.*, Article 26.

20. *Ibid.*, Articles 52, 59.

21. *Ibid.*, Article 52.

22. *Ibid.*, Articles 48-50.

23. *Ibid.*, Articles 59-66.

24. *Ibid.*, Articles 74-84.

25. EEC Commission, *Report on the Execution of the Treaty* (Brussels: EEC, July, 1962), pp. 39-40.

CHAPTER 3 THE THEORY OF ECONOMIC INTEGRATION AND INTRA-EEC TRADE

A major part of the theoretical work in the area of economic integration has been done by four writers: Jacob Viner, James E. Meade, Jan Tinbergen, and Tibor Scitovsky.[1] A number of others have made significant contributions in more limited works dealing with specific aspects of the subject,[2] and most of the essential material on the theory of economic unions has been brought together in two very competent studies by Bela Balassa, and Rolf Sannwald and Jacques Stohler.[3]

Having presented a summary of the trade provisions of the Treaty of Rome relevant to the present study in the preceding section, an attempt will be made at this point to review some of the pertinent theoretical questions posed by economic integration for intra-area trade. Its purpose is threefold: to apply these concepts to the European case, to present a broad framework for the subsequent study of shifts in European trade and production patterns, and to provide a basis for *a priori* statements as to expected changes in these variables. No attempt is made at an exhaustive review of the theory; this has been done elsewhere. Further, the discussion is limited primarily to the "statics" of integration, i.e., the shifts of demand-supply relationships within the community toward an optimization of trade and a maximization of production with given factor endowments and technology. The presumed "dynamic" effects of integration, involving the supply of productive factors and induced changes in economies of scale and technology, will not be dealt with here, although in the long run they may prove to be more significant than static considerations. Necessarily, the material relies heavily upon the work of the above-mentioned authors, among others, although an effort is made to emphasize those ideas which seem especially applicable to the practical problems of evaluating the potential effects of economic unification on the particular phenomena under study here.

TARIFFS AND THE VOLUME AND DIRECTION OF TRADE

For most commodities, national tariffs effectively prevent the international allocation of production to the most efficient suppliers and hence adversely affect world welfare, but not necessarily national welfare.[4] The national markets of high-tariff countries are, via the protective effect of those tariffs, primarily reserved for the domestic producers, since foreign suppliers must add to their basic f.o.b. export price not only the transport costs but also the customs charge before competing in the domestic market. In this way, outside producers are rendered essentially non-competitive with domestic firms on the basis of price. If foreign firms become more efficient, or domestic producers become less so, and if these changes in efficiency are reflected in prices, tariff levels may be adjusted so as to provide the same degree of protection as before. The same thing may be said of the tariff response to changes in relative factor prices.

Protective tariffs, as well as quotas, may be set at levels which provide the precise degree of shielding from foreign competition deemed necessary or desirable by national authorities. As will be shown later, however, tariff levels on many commodities sometimes give little indication of the degree of protection accorded domestic suppliers. This is especially true of certain product categories where a wide variety of pure food and drug regulations, labeling rules, advertising laws, legislated prices, and other restrictions may prevent trade despite the fact that tariffs remain at fairly low levels.

Disregarding the latter exceptions for the moment, it may reasonably be said that the higher the tariffs levels among nations considering participation in an economic union, the greater will be the potential benefit of that union to its members.[5] In a limited case where tariffs among such countries have been prohibitive or where the same effect has been achieved by quotas, and specialization among them is prevented altogether, the potential benefits brought about by an economic union and total abolition of internal tariffs will be great indeed. At the other extreme, where trade among prospective member nations already is essentially free from tariffs and quantitative trade restrictions, the benefits derived by the participating countries from an economic union, all other things equal, should be minimal, and shifts in trade patterns and the volume of trade in response to this development would hardly be expected.[6]

Another aspect of the tariff question, which will be explored in more detail later, is whether the expectation, on the part of businessmen and others, of gradual elimination of internal trade barriers in a customs union causes trade within the union to increase substantially in excess of the trade growth which would be expected on the basis of the individual tariff reductions or quota increases alone. Precisely this assertion has often been made in connection with the EEC: that internal tariff reductions have in fact had little to do with the rapid increase in intra-EEC trade during the first several years of its existence, and that expectations have caused trade growth to _lead_ tariff reductions to a considerable extent.[7]

The formal concepts of trade creation and trade diversion, already implied above, may be brought into the picture at this point.[8] In the absence of tariffs and other trade restrictions, the national market is open to the lowest-cost producers, domestic and foreign. It follows that the imposition of a tariff may lead, in many cases, to a shift in purchases from a low-cost (foreign) producer to a high-cost, protected (domestic) supplier. This is due simply to a shift in the relative prices of the imported and import-competing goods to the domestic consumers or users.

Since, in the formation of a customs union such as the EEC, the tariff walls between one country and all partner countries are eliminated, the discrimination brought about by trade restrictions between domestically produced goods and commodities supplied by manufacturers in other EEC countries is ended, at least on the surface. There presumably results a redistribution of demand-supply relationships within the community tending toward some hypothetical, least-cost optimum. That is, consumers or users seek to purchase all commodities, _ceteris paribus_, from the lowest-cost producers situated within the EEC. This entails a shift from high-cost domestic producers to low-cost suppliers in other member countries, and has been termed the positive production effect.[9]

On the other hand, the above shift to lower-cost suppliers,

which brings with it an increase in over-all productive efficiency and welfare, under these circumstances is strictly limited to the confines of the community. Discrimination still exists between suppliers located within the EEC and suppliers in third countries. Even if the EEC does not cause a rise in external tariffs, the formation of the community will bring about a shift from low-cost suppliers in third countries to high-cost producers in the community. Welfare will suffer, for the same reason as outlined above in connection with national tariffs. This situation has been termed the negative production effect.

Closely related are the so-called positive and negative consumption effects.[10] The shift in consumer and user purchases from domestic to community goods, due to the elimination of discriminatory national tariffs and quotas, is beneficial not only for efficient resource allocation in production as presented above, but also for maximum consumer satisfaction by increasing their effective real incomes. On the other hand, discrimination against third countries' goods in favor of community production induces the opposite, or negative, consumption effects. The former broadens the range of consumer or user choice, while the latter tends to narrow it.

The principal so-called static effects of customs unions thus involve both positive production and consumption effects, resulting in an over-all, once-and-for-all increase in productive efficiency and consumer welfare, and negative consumption and production effects, which have an opposite impact on efficiency and on the economic welfare of consumers or users: trade creation and trade diversion.

If trade barriers among the nations of a customs union have traditionally been prohibitive, one would generally expect trade creation to outweigh trade diversion, with a rapid increase in trade among members, little of which takes place at the expense of imports from third countries.

Applying this general notion to the European scene, one specific approach was suggested as early as 1955.[11] This simply involves an analysis of pre-union tariff structures of the EEC, hypothesizing that all tariffs and quotas were applied on a non-discriminatory basis, and a subsequent comparison of these initial trade restrictions with those that would exist after the substantial completion of the EEC tariff-reduction program. Added to this would be an analysis of differences in production costs among the participating countries since:

> ...the greater the cost differences, the fewer would be the cases of protected domestic industries...as a result of the union.... General knowledge of the economic composition of the area is sufficient to suggest that quite considerable cost differences do exist. Differences in climate, soil, and population diversity; the distribution of coal, iron ore, and other natural resources; and historical factors relating to the geographic concentration of industry, the stock of physical capital, and the supply of skilled labor all suggest possibilities for local specialization within the six countries.[12]

Under high pre-EEC tariffs, producers in member countries could individually have engaged in certain manufacturing activities which, under free trade conditions, might have been impossible due to unfavorable resource endowments or low productivity, and consequent high production costs. After the abolition of internal trade restrictions, the widely divergent endowments of productive factors postulated by Gehrels and Johnston would tend to dictate a considerable shift in production to those suppliers operating at lowest cost; hence the contention that high pre-union tariffs are favorable to the case for economic union. Naturally, if the creation of the union excludes the lowest-cost producer (because he happens to be located in a third country), the benefits of union will be somewhat less, but they will still exist. It is not necessary for the absolute lowest-cost producer of a given commodity to be included in an economic union in order for internal trade in that product to grow, as long as the output of a higher-cost domestic producer is at least partially displaced by a lower-cost foreign producer.

Unlike manufactures, in the case of raw materials little change in EEC trade flows would be expected based on supply costs, since most suppliers are external to the EEC and national tariffs have traditionally been low. Only in coal would such shifts logically be expected.[13] Agricultural production is a special, highly complex case which will not be covered in detail here. On the surface, creation of intra-EEC free trade in agricultural commodities clearly would tend to center production on the efficient farm areas of France and the Netherlands, with German agriculture in many regions of the country turning out to be marginal at best. With national pre-EEC explicit and implicit trade barriers on agricultural commodities being highly protective in virtually every participating country, the expected increase in internal trade in farm produce is substantial, even when the extreme difficulties of liberalization of trade in farm commodities are taken into account.

Once it has been agreed that the higher the pre-union tariff levels, the greater is the potential for expansion of intra-union trade, the problem of estimating the restrictive effect of such pre-union tariffs must be dealt with.[14] One possibility would be to simply take an unweighted average of all national tariff positions and, by comparing the results for the various countries under study, decide which are protectionist and which have pursued relatively liberal trade policies. On the other hand, each tariff position could be weighted by the import quantity and an average taken of the results. However, since almost no goods are imported under extremely high tariffs, the weighting process would probably turn out to be entirely misleading.

Prior to the formation of the EEC, the use of unweighted mean tariffs in analysis of national tariff structures was not common practice in Europe. While one country would separate a certain product category into twenty tariff positions, another country would impose only one duty rate on the entire product group. Hence this particular goods category would be counted twenty times in computing the unweighted arithmetic mean of all tariff positions in the first country, while it would be counted only once in the second case, thereby severely impeding comparability between the two mean tariff levels.[15] Two factors have, however, served to reduce distortions brought about by differing customs policies. First, tariff nomenclature and practices in Western Europe underwent considerable harmonization during the 1950-60 period, most significantly after the beginnings of European economic integration with the European Coal and Steel Community in 1953. Second, European countries in tariff classification generally subdivide industrial product groups more, and raw materials categories less. Since tariffs on industrial products are generally higher than duties on semi-processed goods and raw materials, this practice results in an upward bias in the average tariff level of all European countries, but it does not impede the comparability of the individual national mean tariff levels.

Theoretically, it would be useful to supplement the unweighted mean tariff with its respective frequency distributions.[16] For example, although both country A and country B might have an unweighted mean tariff of 10 per cent, all of country A's tariffs might lie between 12 per cent and 8 per cent while country B's tariffs might be dispersed between, say, 80 per cent and 5 per cent. Necessarily, the protective effect of a given unweighted mean tariff level would also be somewhat affected by the nature of the corresponding frequency distribution of tariffs. Nevertheless, most authors in the literature as well as the EEC authorities seem to be content with the unweighted mean tariff as a sufficiently reliable indicator of the degree of protection involved. Moreover, since the comparison of tariffs by means of frequency distributions would entail commodity-by-commodity analyses, the highly valued "across the board" principle of EEC integration would almost certainly be sacrificed at least partially, and it is doubtful whether such analysis would change the picture materially. Unweighted averages of tariffs will also be utilized in the remainder of this study. Similarly, the 1957 Rome Treaty employs unweighted means of the members' national tariff levels to arrive at the common external tariff for the entire community. Referring to the preceding chapter, it is easy to see how this procedure results in a raising of the low BLEU and Dutch tariffs against third countries, and a lowering of the French and Italian duties, with German tariff levels remaining about the same.

Turning briefly to some aspects of the creation of the EEC within the larger framework of the trading world as a whole, negative production and consumption effects, as described earlier, imply the diversion of trade with third countries to trade with member countries. For third countries, these "trade-diverting" effects are vastly more significant than the trade-creating influences. The latter deal almost exclusively with internal shifts in supply relationships and have little to do with the external economic relations of the community. Only to the extent that increased efficiency and welfare within the EEC, brought about by internal trade-creation, is accompanied by a rise in national income in the member countries will external trade relationships be affected.

Trade-diverting effects, on the other hand, do have a direct bearing upon EEC trade with third countries. The magnitude of this real or potential discrimination against extra-EEC suppliers has been the subject of widespread study and conjecture, although we will not deal with it further here.

The present study is primarily concerned with the "statics" of economic integration. However, it is possible that the formation of the European Economic Community has resulted in a more rapid rise in the national income of the partner countries than would have been the case in the absence of economic integration for another reason. This involves an increased rate of investment, a higher rate of technological change, inter-country and inter-regional flows of productive factors, the introduction of economies of scale, and other elements making for more rapid economic growth. Normally, any increase in national income is accompanied by a greater demand for imports. This is not likely to be different in the case of the EEC, and on this basis alone increased trade with the rest of the world might be expected. Nevertheless, for some commodities the static, trade-diverting effects are likely to predominate over the trade expansion induced by rising incomes. Whether trade diversion or trade expansion will, in the final analysis, be the net result for a variety of traded commodities, with respect to the outside world, is the basic question which concerns non-EEC countries in both the developed and the underdeveloped areas.

On the basis of the above theoretical arguments, what would be the *a priori* effects on intra-EEC trade of the gradual elimination of trade restrictions among the member countries? To the extent that substantial per-unit cost differences exist among producers of manufactured goods within the community, tariff reductions would be expected to greatly increase the volume of trade in manufactures among the member nations: On the one hand, low-cost community suppliers will displace sales of high-cost suppliers in their domestic markets. In addition, the accompanying price decline will stimulate the aggregate quantity demanded of the goods in question and this incremental demand will to a large extent be satisfied by these same low-cost EEC suppliers.[17]

Similarly, intra-EEC trade in finished and semi-finished components would also be expected to grow substantially. Partially, this may be attributed to the expected increase in final demand for manufactures and the consequent growth in materials input requirements. On the other hand, reduced tariffs on the intermediate goods themselves would be expected to raise trade volumes within the EEC according to the same reasoning applied to manufactures above.

But a significant increase in the annual volume of trade among the member countries of the Common Market may be by no means the most important potential end-result of the EEC internal trade liberalization program. Rather, growth of intra-EEC trade as a direct result of the removal of trade restrictions among the participating economies points to a redistribution of production in favor of the lower-cost suppliers within the framework of the community at large.[18] Clearly, the greater the initial per-unit cost differences, i.e., those existing at the inception of the EEC, among suppliers in the various member nations, the more extensive will be the degree of this shifting of production patterns.

A priori reasoning indicates that, as tariff protection from intra-EEC price competition is gradually reduced, high-cost producers necessarily would have to strive to meet the prices of imports. Some high-cost suppliers will be unsuccessful in meeting the new import competition and will be forced out of the market. The domestic market served by these marginal suppliers will then be satisfied by imports; and production, within the EEC, of the commodity in question will be shifted to lower-cost suppliers in the exporting country.

In the case of certain goods it is not unreasonable to expect abrupt short-term shifts in the locus of production such as those outlined above within the EEC: High-cost domestic producers are forced out of the market over a relatively short period of time and domestic output is replaced by imports. Much more likely, however, is the case where imports force the domestic prices downward to a point where all fixed costs of producers are no longer being fully covered. These firms will then be forced to withdraw, and their share of the domestic market taken over by imports, thereby shifting the locus of production of the commodity in question in favor of low-cost EEC suppliers, although somewhat more gradually.

Alternatively, if the high-cost suppliers are able to meet the newly created import competition by themselves lowering production costs via increased efficiency, there may be no shifts in the locus of production at all. No intra-area trade will have been created by the removal of internal tariffs, which is attributable to the reallocation of production. Yet integration would have served the purpose of enhancing productive efficiency just as surely as if it had in fact caused widespread shifts in the locus of production.

On top of this, we have seen earlier that the downward pressure on prices presumably caused by internal tariff reductions and the enhanced import competition they bring about will raise the quantity demanded of the good concerned. This increase in domestic demand, whether gradual or short-term, will also be met by imports from low-cost EEC suppliers. Assuming no income-effects of integration, the extent of this rise in the quantity demanded depends entirely upon the price elasticity of demand for the commodity in question.

Clearly, there are also factors which militate against free competition on an over-all EEC scale even if the reduction of customs duties are sufficient to substantially remove tariff barriers. These have been largely enumerated elsewhere in this study.[19] To the extent that such explicit or implicit non-tariff barriers to trade are effective in preventing the free interplay of competitive forces, the increase in the value of intra-EEC trade and, more importantly, the redistribution of production will be correspondingly less. Wide differences in the protective power of national turnover tax rebates and countervailing duties, national fiscal levies imposed exclusively on imports, protective technical and procedural import regulations, and extensive government-sponsored "buy domestic" campaigns are examples in this category. Finally, subsidies in various forms accorded domestic producers also may prevent such competitive shifts in the patterns of trade and production in the EEC. Such subsidies are difficult to pinpoint both because they are usually well disguised and because of the widespread government ownership of, or participation in, certain segments of EEC industry.

We assume here that non-tariff protective factors and subsidies have been secondary to the tariffs themselves. If this is in fact true, then intra-EEC tariff reductions during the first eight years of the community should have brought about a significant rise in the volume of internal trade and at least some degree of reallocation of production among member countries.[20]

On the other hand, a number of considerations other than the removal of trade restrictions may serve to enhance the rate of intra-EEC trade growth as well as shifts in the locus of production. Already in 1961, commenting on the EEC internal trade situation, the OECD stated:

> Although the rate of expansion in trade between the EEC countries was slower than in 1960, it continued the trend toward rapid integration of the markets of the six member countries, stimulated to some extent by the tariff reductions granted by these countries to each other, but probably even more by industry's deliberate cultivation of the area as if it were already a single market. The increase in trade, however, did not bring out any clear evidence thus far about significant shifts in the localization of industry inside the community.[21]

Of the non-tariff reasons which led to the expectation of rapid trade growth in the EEC, three are perhaps most important. First, it is generally well known that the first six years of economic integration in the Common Market took place in a climate of rapid rise in economic activity in all of the member countries, without exception. Referring to the concept of marginal propensity to import, increases in economic activity in a country almost invariably bring with them a rise in the demand for imports. Moreover, a country with a relatively low <u>average</u> propensity to import (e.g., France or Italy) may face a fairly high <u>marginal</u> propensity to import. Significant increases in real per-capita income may lead to a demand for goods not available in quantity domestically and cause a rapid rise in imports and, if the previous low level of imports consisted mainly of raw materials and capital goods, the marginal propensity to import will be relatively high.[22] Further, it is not unreasonable to expect that such marginal imports will be supplied to a considerable extent by EEC partner countries, although this conclusion must be modified by the nature of supply conditions in exporting member nations.

Secondly, various types of business agreements may serve to expand intra-EEC trade considerably in excess of that which might be expected as a result of reductions in trade barriers. Subsidiaries, mergers, and licensing agreements spread over the Common Market area may have tended to increase trade in components, intermediate goods, and capital equipment even before this trade would have been expected to develop as a result of tariff reductions.

Finally, we have already indicated that expectations on the part of businessmen of a fully integrated market within ten or twelve years might lead to highly intensified promotion and sales efforts by firms in all EEC nations throughout the Common Market. These efforts to create or extend the market for a particular good may stimulate widespread demand for the item where little or none existed before, due perhaps to insufficient knowledge. Enormous gains in tourism throughout the EEC by residents of the member countries must have accelerated this development to some degree.

Already in 1959, the United Nations Economic Commission for Europe issued a general *a priori* statement regarding the probable effects on trade and on the locus of production in the EEC as a result of internal tariff reductions:[23]

> While some confidence may be felt in the long-term beneficial effects of the formation of the Common Market... on members as a group, the benefits may be very unevenly distributed among individual countries. The low-tariff countries clearly have the best chance to extend their export markets in countries where tariffs are at present high without having to face significantly increased competition in their home markets. By contrast, a country which has succeeded in turning the terms of trade in its favour may face some loss of this advantage when its home market is opened to the competition of industry in other member countries. On the other hand, such a country may well have more to gain in the long run than has a low-tariff country from the stimulating effects of competition on industrial enterprise and efficiency, and from the transfer of resources from less to more productive uses which may be forced upon it.
>
> A further factor tending to make the long-term benefits of the Common Market... fall unevenly on their members is the possibility that the important changes in industrial location likely to result from it will reinforce tendencies toward industrial concentration and centralization.

> Many new industrial plants are likely to be set up, including both those of European enterprises seeking to realize the advantage of large-scale production, and the direct investment of overseas firms seeking to establish themselves inside the new preferential area.

While the removal of intra-EEC tariffs and other trade restrictions, or the expectations thereof, perhaps assumes the predominant role in theoretical analyses of shifts in trade and production patterns, other considerations must be taken into account as well. Economic distance among participating countries, complementarity and competitiveness in the range of goods produced by the respective economies, as well as other questions of some theoretical significance to economic integration of the Common Market countries, are presented below.

COMPLEMENTARITY AND COMPETITIVENESS

The degree of competition, or rivalry, which exists between two or more economies before the creation of a customs union has often been considered one factor which is likely to affect the potential benefits of such a union. Competitiveness and complementarity have been defined both in terms of product range and comparative costs.

In the former case, two economies are said to be competitive if there exists a considerable degree of overlapping in the range of goods produced in the two countries by industries sheltered from import competition by protective tariffs.[24] This holds whether or not the goods are exported and actually do compete on world markets. Conversely, complementarity would characterize the two economies if there exists a great deal of differentiation in the scope of production. For example, the Danish and the German economies would be considered complementary--Denmark to some degree specializes in the production of agricultural commodities while German output is characterized predominantly by industrial goods. On the other hand, the German and British economies might be described as being primarily competitive in nature: Both are highly industrialized and produce a similar range of goods.

The second, perhaps more recent, definition of

competitiveness and complementarity is quite different. Two economies are said to be complementary whenever there exist substantial differences in production costs between them for most goods produced, and competitive whenever production costs are approximately equal.[25] Hence the American and the Japanese economies might be considered complementary and the German and the Dutch economies could be considered competitive. Under this definition, a customs union between complementary economies would seem to be more beneficial, since production would necessarily shift from high-cost producers in one country to the low-cost suppliers in the other nation (assuming zero economic distance and constant costs) if both countries produced a given commodity before the formation of the union. Two major criticisms which may be leveled at this definition of complementarity and competitiveness are the lack of a really adequate basis for comparing costs internationally and continuous changes which tend to occur in cost structures over time, thereby negating the assumption of constant costs.[26]

Viner's more workable concept of competitiveness does, in fact, appear to contain an implicit recognition of cost differences, although the problem seems to be considerably more complex than this. Since the institution of the EEC, the removal of internal tariffs on automobiles, for instance, has resulted in a rapid expansion of trade in this good between France and Germany. It is apparent, however, that very little of this trade growth is traceable to cost differences: Product quality and tastes seem to account for most of it. French manufacturers of passenger cars have been able to capture a respectable share of the West German market, despite the fact that the c.i.f. price difference in Germany between imports from France and domestic output is minor. In contrast, German auto producers seem to have made a comparatively poor showing in the French market, largely because the design of the product often has little appeal to French tastes. In contrast, expanded intra-EEC trade in certain other consumer durables has been primarily due to price differences and shifts from high-cost to low-cost producers (e.g., refrigerators).

Generalizing on the Vinerian definition of competitiveness and complementarity, then, the more complementary are the economies facing integration (i.e., the less the degree of overlapping of their respective outputs), the less will be the potential benefits of such integration. Hence, integration between the U.K. and Portugal, for example, would yield relatively few benefits for either country, and would probably tend toward discrimination against third countries and toward economic self-sufficiency. Any increase in trade between complementary economies due to integration will occur primarily at the expense of imports from third countries.

Conversely, the greater the competitiveness, or rivalry, between such economies prior to integration, the greater will be the potential benefits. Initial tariffs between such economies will be relatively high and their removal will lead to a shift from high-cost to low-cost producers within the union. Everything else being equal, marginal firms will be eliminated and production will increasingly be concentrated on the most efficient firms in the economic union. Moreover, the larger the pre-union differences in costs, the greater will be the consequent increase in efficiency. Intra-union trade will increase rapidly and discrimination against outside suppliers in the form of decreased imports will be relatively minor. Even when cost differences are unimportant, integration of competitive economies will increase the range of choice of consumers or users and thereby presumably enhance their economic well-being.

Applying this concept to the European case, a glance at the qualitative makeup of production in the five EEC economies (BLEU, France, Germany, Italy, and the Netherlands) reveals competitiveness, or rivalry, to clearly be the dominant characteristic.[27] Virtually every industrial and agricultural good is produced in significant amounts in two or more of the member countries. Furthermore, perhaps the only commodity groups which might be considered predominantly complementary to the EEC economy--most raw materials and a large number of tropical and sub-tropical agricultural products--have long been supplied by nations not directly included in the EEC.[28] Hence on the basis of competitiveness and complementarity alone, one would be led to expect substantial growth in internal trade; at the same time, all other things equal, little of this increase in the volume of internal trade, based on rivalry or competitiveness, should take place at the expense of imports from third countries.

On the other hand, the EFTA (European Free Trade Association) seems to be characterized comparatively less by competitiveness and more by complementarity than the EEC. Traditional British imports of agricultural commodities from Scandinavia, and exports of industrial goods to these northern countries, should be little affected by the formation of a free trade area. Similar, relatively complementary relationships also seem to exist, although perhaps to a somewhat lesser degree, between the U.K. and Ireland, Austria, Switzerland, and Portugal. Hence one would expect the increase in EFTA internal trade to be correspondingly less than intra-EEC trade growth, with a concomitant increase in the danger of discrimination against suppliers in third countries.

A substantial degree of complementarity also seems to exist in the LAFTA (Latin American Free Trade Association), although other factors play a somewhat more important role in limiting the potential effectiveness of this union.[29] On the other hand, complementarity actually is striven for in the Soviet Bloc COMECON in an attempt to reallocate production to least-cost suppliers through "socialistic division of labor." This is supposed to achieve the same ultimate goal as that which competition is designed to attain in the "social market economy" of the EEC. However, many doubts have been expressed that the administrative allocation of production among the participating countries will in fact lead to some sort of least-cost optimum.[30] The Association of the EEC with the participating African nations and territories, Greece, and Turkey seems to be substantially more complementary than competitive. Increases in the volume of trade among the EEC and the associated countries due to shifts in the locus of production are likely to be negligible, and discrimination against non-member countries may be considerable.[31]

ECONOMIC SIZE AND DISTANCE

Another means of attempting to determine, on an a priori basis, the potential effects of an economic union upon internal and external trade of the member countries is the analysis of the absolute size of that union in economic terms. A great deal has been written on this particular subject and considerable divergence of opinion exists, even in the most recent literature.

Perhaps the most plausible argument holds that the greater the economic area of a union, the greater will be the possibility for extensive reallocation of production in favor of the lowest-cost suppliers.[33] The probability that the low-cost producers will be included in a given customs union naturally increases as the absolute size of the union increases to include more and more producing units. Following this argument to its logical conclusion, the elimination of all trade restrictions in the world (i.e., the creation, in a sense, of a world-wide customs union) would lead ceteris paribus to optimum division of labor and efficiency among all countries. This reasoning seems to hold even without the introduction of economies of scale due to increased market size, increased production, and other so-called dynamic factors accompanying economic integration.

To illustrate, suppose countries X and Y both produce radios for their limited domestic markets and impose high protective tariffs to keep out imports. Country Z also produces radios but at a much lower cost than X or Y. It applies a negligible, or zero, tariff and competes actively on world markets for the product. Suppose further that a customs union were contemplated between X and Y. Since both national radio industries produce at high cost relative to Z, and since cost differences are presumed to be slight, we would expect very little increase in trade of radios between the two nations after all barriers have been removed (assuming no trade induced by differences in quality or tastes). Hence the potential benefit of such a union, at least in this area, is slight.

If, on the other hand, the union is extended to include country Z, internal trade in radios would develop rapidly and production would shift from the high-cost suppliers in X and Y to the more efficient producers in Z. Indeed, if most producers in X and Y turn out to be marginal, radio production in these two countries would be sharply curtailed. Otherwise, they would be forced to step up efficiency in production to the point where they would be competitive with suppliers in Z. In this case, total production in all probability also would rise.

The latter conclusion was reached by Tinbergen by means of a mathematical model showing that each increase in the size of a union under such circumstances would increase total output and productive efficiency.[34] If, however, the increase in size of the union induces widespread changes in economic policy or includes nations with vastly different economic structures, these conclusions will not necessarily hold.

This latter point is especially emphasized by Wilhelm Roepke, who maintains that, whereas small nations are almost always interested in world-wide trade liberalization, this is not necessarily true of large nations (or customs unions).[35] While Denmark or Switzerland needs free access to world markets in order to maintain efficient, low-cost production and high incomes, the United States and the Soviet Union do not. Hence the larger the economic size, the less would be the interest in promoting world trade and the greater would be the danger of policies favoring economic self-sufficiency. On the basis of the actions of EEC officials during 1960-64, one could be led to believe that such arguments partially serve to explain the formulation of Common Market trade policy, although the future development of EEC commercial policy may not substantiate them.

The measurement of market size is itself open to considerable argument. In order to develop a reasonably valid measure for this purpose, each increase in market size should bring with it a high probability that more and more competing firms and industries will be included in the extension of the economic area. Population as a measure of economic size has been rejected on the grounds that it fails to indicate the possibilities for division of labor which we are seeking, and Gross National Product seems to be a more suitable indicator for market size. Hence it may be said that the greater the GNP of an economic union, the greater are the possibilities for division of labor and internal specialization within that union.[36]

However, the criterion of economic size is hardly sufficient by itself. We will see later that the effective size of the market is, to a great extent, determined by the level of transportation costs and the nature of the transport system. Similarly, great heterogeneity in tastes may also tend to limit market size. For instance, a great many domestic products appeal predominantly to domestic tastes, and extension of the size of the customs union would do little to increase the size of the market facing the suppliers of such commodities. Unquestionably, neither of these limiting factors is entirely exogenous; and both may be overcome or lessened in time through construction of efficient transport facilities, increased tourism, and consumer education programs, the latter forces themselves partly arising out of the economic integration.

Finally, differences in measurement standards, specifications and business practices also may to some extent limit the economic area facing producers in a customs union despite the absence of explicit trade barriers. For example, problems of this nature would be the concern of suppliers in both the U.K. and the EEC if Britain were to join the Common Market: Whereas the metric system is used exclusively in all of the EEC countries, Britain still retains the English system and this could pose problems for the rapid expansion of intra-area trade in the event of British entry. Nevertheless, such difficulties probably would resolve themselves once integration has proceeded to any substantial degree.

In general, abstracting from the above problems, the potential for specialization and expanded internal trade in a customs union is greater, the larger the economic size of that union, measured in terms of GNP. Hence it would be expected that the economic benefits of the EEC exceed those of the smaller EFTA which, in turn, exceed those of the Benelux union. Drawing on this conclusion, the potential benefits of economic integration in Latin America, Southeast Asia, or East Africa could be quite limited.

Another indicator of the potential influence of a customs union on trade and production patterns which may be useful, especially for an initial analysis, is economic distance. As formulated by Jacob Viner, among others, this proposition states that increased trade and division of labor within an economic union will be greater, the smaller the economic distance between member nations of that union.[37]

Economic distance, as a concept, is probably most useful when it is defined in terms of transportation costs. However, differences in customs and tastes--the character of the people--which occur over geographical distance have also been employed in this connection. Although the special element is often absent from international trade theory, it is valuable here as a force affecting the potential shifts in trade flows and production patterns as a result of economic integration.

In general, allocation of production according to the dictates of either the classical theory of comparative costs or the factor endowments doctrine can be brought about only in the complete absence of transportation costs. The higher the costs of transport among suppliers of a given commodity, *ceteris paribus*, the less likely will be the allocation of production to the lowest-cost suppliers: If transportation costs between two countries are prohibitive, there can be no real competition among suppliers in those countries and trade will be virtually nonexistent.

In a customs union as well, the higher the transportation costs within the union, the less will be its potential benefits. Natural obstacles such as mountain ranges, jungles, and swamps, as well as the prevailing mode of transportation, clearly influence economic distance. Although the geographical distances may be small, economic distances may be large. For instance, the economic distance between Santos, Brazil, and a large number of Brazilian inland points may be greater than the economic distance between Santos and New York or Rotterdam, even though the geographical distance is far smaller in the former case. On the basis of economic distance in this sense, all else being equal, the EEC may be considered potentially more beneficial than an economic union of certain Latin American or African nations. Similarly, if the geographic as well as the economic distance between widely dispersed EFTA countries can be shown to be greater than between the closely knit EEC member states, the former also appears potentially less beneficial.

If economic distance is presumed to be a factor affecting the usefulness of an economic union, a means of estimating this distance must be devised. Such a measure must then be expressed in monetary terms to reflect the transport cost of trade between actual or potential member countries. Probably the most practicable solution to this problem simply involves subtracting the f.o.b. value of goods being exported to other member states from their c.i.f. value upon entry into the importing countries. The difference will indicate the cost of transportation, handling, and insurance for each good involved in intra-union trade.[38]

There is little doubt that price changes which occur while commodities are in transit, divergent product classification, and similar factors may impair the validity of such estimates to some degree, depending upon the nature of the good concerned. Nevertheless, Beckerman's use of this indicator--correlating economic distance with the volume of trade--seems to have been fairly successful, showing a high rank correlation among Western European nations. Similarly, Balassa's application of substantially the same technique to Western Europe seems to show that--based on economic distance alone--a customs union including the BLEU, France, Germany, and the Netherlands would be most advantageous. When Italy, the sixth member of the EEC, is included, the advantage declines considerably, more so, in fact, than if the U.K., Switzerland, and Austria joined the above five countries in an economic union.[39]

The application of such a criterion to the Latin American case, with far less developed transportation systems and formidable natural barriers to trade, serves to point out some of the difficulties with which LAFTA is faced.[40] Similarly, customs unions undertaken or contemplated in Southeast Asia and Africa seem to offer somewhat limited promise of potential benefit to the member nations if only due to the lack of adequate transportation facilities needed for the efficient international exchange of goods. Nevertheless, the intensive development of conventional transportation systems and the creation of new means of transport in these areas may eventually change the picture substantially.

Another application of the idea of propinquity to economic integration centers around differences in tastes, national character, and customs. If two countries are vastly different in the tastes and character of their respective peoples, one might expect the degree of trade between them to grow relatively less rapidly than between two more similar nations, after the elimination of trade barriers.[41] Nevertheless, it is possible, if not probable, that the greater the degree of industrialization of the participating countries, the less will be the importance of such factors. Industrialization and the growth of personal disposable income appears to foster the development of similar demand patterns on the part of consumers, no matter what their socio-historical background may be. Likewise, all industrialized countries require substantially the same types of capital equipment, which varies little, whether it be imported or manufactured domestically. Differences in national character thus may have had little negative influence upon the integration of the French, Italian, and German economies even though the three nations have in the past differed substantially in this regard. In the case of less developed countries, especially in Asia, such a conclusion may not necessarily hold. Especially in agricultural commodities, trade may to some extent be impeded by differences in national tastes, at least in the short run.

Finally, it might be thought that nations which have traditionally been political enemies are relatively unsuited partners in an economic union. This argument presupposes that national sentiments are not susceptible to change in a relatively short time period. However, numerous, rapid shifts in military alliances throughout modern history seem to refute this point of view, as does the close cooperation in most areas between Germany and her former enemies in the EEC and other European projects. Serious problems have, in fact, arisen during the process of integration in the EEC, but there is little evidence to support the notion that such problems are traceable to traditional ill-feeling between the participating national states.[42]

In this chapter, then, we have attempted to point out some of the theoretical arguments relating to economic integration in Europe and to present several predictions as to changes in the patterns of trade and production which these ideas imply. None of the factors mentioned can be isolated as to its impact on the EEC: Each factor has at least some bearing on one or more of the others and itself may be influenced to a greater or lesser degree by economic integration.

Notes to Chapter 3

1. Jacob Viner, The Customs Union Issue (New York: Carnegie Endowment for International Peace, 1950);
James E. Meade, The Theory of Customs Unions (Amsterdam: North Holland Publishing Company, 1955), and Problems of Economic Union (Chicago: University of Chicago Press, 1953);
Jan Tinbergen, International Economic Integration (2nd ed.; Amsterdam: Elsevier, 1965);
Tibor Scitovsky, Economic Theory and Western European Integration (Stanford: Stanford University Press, 1958).

2. Especially: Franz Gehrels, "Customs Unions From a Single-Country Viewpoint," Review of Economic Studies, 1956-57;
R.G. Lipsey, "The Theory of Customs Unions: A

General Survey," Economic Journal, September, 1960; and
H. Mankower and G. Morton, "A Contribution to the Theory of Customs Unions," Economic Journal, March, 1953.

3. Bela Balassa, The Theory of Economic Integration (Homewood, Ill.: Richard D. Irwin, 1962);
Rolf Sannwald and Jacques Stohler, Economic Integration (Princeton: Princeton University Press, 1959).

4. See especially: Tibor Scitovsky, "A Reconsideration of the Theory of Tariffs," in American Economic Association Readings on the Theory of International Trade (Homewood, Ill.: Richard D. Irwin, 1949), pp. 358-89; and
James E. Meade, Trade and Welfare (London: Oxford University Press, 1955), Chapter X.

5. Viner, op. cit., pp. 51-52.

6. The response of the volume of inter-country trade to the imposition or abolition of national tariff barriers clearly depends upon the relevant price elasticities of demand for, and supply of, traded and non-traded goods prevailing in the respective countries.

7. See, for example, United Nations, Economic Survey of Europe, 1959.

8. Viner, op. cit., supra.

9. See Harry G. Johnson, "The European Common Market: Risk or Opportunity?" Weltwirtschaftliches Archiv, No. 2 (1957), pp. 267-68.

10. Ibid.

11. Franz Gehrels and Bruce F. Johnston, "The Economic Gains of European Integration," Journal of Political Economy, Vol. LXIII (August, 1955), pp. 279-81.

12. Ibid., pp. 279-80.

13. See Louis Lister, Europe's Coal and Steel Community (New York: Twentieth Century Fund, 1960).

14. See Hans-Christoph Binswanger, "Der Zollschutz in

den Laendern der Europaeischen Wirtschaftsgemeinschaft und in der Schweiz," in Die europaeische Wirtschaftsintegration im Banne des Gemeinsamen Marktes (Zurich: Polygraphischer Verlag, 1959), pp. 119-51.

15. R. Bertrand, "Comparison du niveau des tarifs duaniers des pays du Marché Commun" (Paris: Institut de Science Economique Appliqué, 1958), p. 11.

16. The question is discussed more fully in Chapter 4.

17. See K. Kermann, Europas handelswirtschaftliche Einheit (Baden-Baden: August Lutzeyer, 1960).

18. See G. Marcey, "How Far Can Foreign Trade and Customs Agreements Confer Upon Small Nations the Advantages of Large Nations?" in E. A. G. Robinson (ed.), Economic Consequences of the Size of Nations (London: Macmillan, 1960), pp. 265-81, especially pp. 270-72.

19. See Chapter 4.

20. Partial justification of this notion in the case of the Low Countries may be found in P. J. Verdoorn, "The Intra-Bloc Trade of the Benelux," in E. A. G. Robinson (ed.), Economic Consequences of the Size of Nations (London: Macmillan, 1960), pp. 291-329.

21. Organization for Economic Cooperation and Development, International Trade, 1961 (Paris: OECD, 1962), p. 83.

22. Jaroslav Vanek, International Trade: Theory and Economic Policy (Homewood, Ill.: Richard D. Irwin, 1962), p. 125.

23. United Nations, Economic Commission for Europe, Economic Survey of Europe, 1959 (Geneva: U.N., 1960), Chapter IV, p. 17.

24. Viner, op. cit., supra.

25. See especially H. Mankower and G. Morton, "A Contribution Toward a Theory of Customs Unions," Economic Journal, March, 1953, pp. 33-49.

26. Balassa, op. cit., p. 31.

27. See, for example, data on the composition of industrial and agricultural output of the EEC countries in United Nations, Statistical Office, Monthly Bulletin of Statistics; or Europa Publications, Ltd, Europa Yearbook, various issues, 1953-65 inclusive.

28. This does not apply, of course, when the Associated Overseas Countries and Territories, affiliated with the EEC, are included.

29. See Miguel S. Wionczek, "Latin American Free Trade Association," International Conciliation, January, 1965.

30. See, for example, Andrzej Korbonski, "Comecon," International Conciliation, September, 1964;
R. Krenzel, "Die wirtschaftlichen Integrationsbestrebungen und Integrationshindernisse im Ostblock," in E. Boettcher (ed.), Ostblock, EWG und Entwicklungslaender (Stuttgart: W. Kohlhammer, 1963), pp. 55-79; and
F. L. Pryor, The Communist Foreign Trade System (Cambridge: MIT Press, 1963).

31. Paul Erdmann and Peter Rogge, Die Europaeische Wirtschaftsgemeinschaft und die Drittlaender (Basel: Kylos-Verlag, 1960).

32. Viner, op. cit., Chapter IV;
Jan Tinbergen, Selected Papers (Amsterdam: North Holland Publishing Company, 1959), pp. 152-64;
Balassa, op. cit., pp. 35-39.

33. Viner, op. cit., p. 51.

34. Tinbergen, op. cit., supra, p. 164.

35. In "Gemeinsamer Markt und Freihandelszone," Ordo, 1958.

36. Balassa, op. cit., p. 36.

37. See especially Viner, op. cit., Chapter VIII.

38. See W. Beckerman, "Distance and Pattern in

Intra-European Trade," Review of Economics and Statistics, February, 1956.

39. Balassa, op. cit., pp. 42-43.

40. Wionczek, op. cit., pp. 35-38.

41. This notion has been applied to general trade theory by Staffan B. Linder in An Essay on Trade and Transformation (Stockholm: Almquist & Wicksell, 1961), pp. 94-101.

42. Problems which might be mentioned in this regard that have developed during the first six years of the EEC relate especially to agriculture, social policies, relations with third countries, and the regulation of competition.

CHAPTER 4 CHANGE IN INTRA-EEC TRADE RESTRICTIONS

The two preceding chapters have presented a general discussion of the formal trade provisions included in the Treaty of Rome and the extent of their implementation during the period under consideration. They have also outlined the general direction of change in intra-community trade and production patterns which is indicated by the theoretical work that has been done in the field of economic integration. The present chapter describes the de facto reduction of trade barriers within the Common Market during 1958-65. We need to know what happened to tariffs, quotas, and other trade restrictions before embarking on a study of the impact which these changes presumably exercised upon trade and production patterns.

During the 1958-65 period, the reduction of tariffs within the EEC was substantial. By the end of 1965, they had been reduced to 30 per cent of the rates in force at the beginning of 1957. Under the Common Market system of periodic 10 per cent tariff cuts outlined in Chapter 2, it is clear that the highest-tariff countries would have to submit to the most significant reductions in import duties. For example, the EEC nation possessing the highest pre-Common Market mean tariff on a cross-section of twenty-eight import categories was Italy, with an unweighted mean duty of 25.5 per cent ad valorem.[1] Consequently, each of the six 10 per cent intra-EEC tariff cuts during the 1958-64 period meant a reduction of 2.55 per cent in the Italian duty. The corresponding figures for France, Germany, and the Benelux countries are 2.4, 1.0, and 0.9, respectively.[2]

During 1958-65, the unweighted arithmetic mean of Italian duties on these twenty-eight import categories was reduced from 25.5 per cent to 7.7 per cent. France, almost as protectionist as Italy, reduced its mean duty from 24 per cent to 7.2 per cent at the end of 1965. Germany, which had already lowered its tariffs considerably prior to the formation of the EEC, mainly in order to discourage price and wage increases during a period of rapid rise in economic activity, lowered the average of its duties from 10 per cent in 1959 to 3 per cent at the end of 1965. The Benelux countries have traditionally levied comparatively low import duties due to their dependence upon imports for a large number of raw materials, capital equipment, and consumer goods categories. Consequently, the decrease in Benelux duties as a result of the Common Market tariff program was relatively smaller than those of the remaining member countries: from 9 per cent in 1957 to 2.7 per cent at the end of 1965. Most striking was the initial difference in mean tariff levels between the high-tariff countries on the one hand, and the Benelux countries and Germany on the other hand, which prevailed at the inception of the EEC tariff program in 1958.

These initial mean tariff levels seem to have been closely related to the respective nations' dependence upon foreign trade as measured, however roughly, by the national average ratio of imports to GNP: the average propensity to import. Those countries highly dependent upon foreign trade for the level and growth of real per capita income, with a substantial degree of specialization in the range of goods produced, generally possess the highest average propensity to import.[3] As a result of this dependence on foreign trade, these same countries usually maintain the most liberal trade restrictions against imports. Table 1 presents the average propensities to import of the present EEC member nations for four selected years prior to the formation of the Common Market. Comparison of these figures and the tariff levels presented in Table 2 clearly shows this similarity to exist, with the possible exception of West Germany.

Table 1

Pre-EEC Average Propensities to Import of Five EEC Countries[4]

Country	1948	1950	1952	1956
Belgium	37	37	40	37
France	12	15	15	11
Germany	n. a.	16	16	14
Netherlands	39	50	48	45
Italy	14	14	18	17

If tariffs were in fact the primary force preventing trade between the EEC nations, then it would follow that, ceteris paribus, the growth of intra-EEC imports, both in quantity and value, would be most rapid in the case of Italy and least rapid in the case of the traditionally low-tariff Benelux countries during the 1958-65 period under construction.

DISTRIBUTION OF THE TARIFFS

It has been asserted that the unweighted arithmetic average of all duty positions[5] of a given national tariff structure alone cannot convey sufficient information about the degree of protection embodied in that tariff wall. Rather, the distribution of tariff positions about the arithmetic mean must be taken into consideration as well. As regards manufactured imports, for instance, a national tariff wall of 20 per cent levied on each and every import is considerably less protective than a tariff structure where the individual duties are distributed evenly between 0 and 40 per cent, with the lowest duties falling on raw materials and, say, tropical agricultural imports. Since the lowest tariffs are, in fact, generally levied on raw materials and agricultural commodities, it may be stated that, in general, the wider the distribution of tariffs about the mean (or median), the greater will be the protective power of that tariff structure. Hence the so-called low-tariff EEC member countries enumerated earlier may not really have possessed significantly less protective tariff structures than the high mean tariff member countries, if it can be demonstrated that their tariffs were considerably more widely distributed.

H. C. Binswanger carried through an interesting analysis on the distribution of tariffs prior to the formation of the EEC for the Common Market countries and Switzerland, using the median tariff rate for each country as the measure of central tendency and upper and lower quartile values to indicate the degree of dispersion.[6] Fifty per cent of all tariffs fall between the upper and lower quartiles and, if the upper quartile tariff is only slightly higher than the lower quartile value, at least half of all tariffs must fall close to the median, and the distribution will be fairly narrow. As an indicator of the deviation of tariffs from his measure of central tendency, the median, this author employed the difference between the upper and lower quartiles divided by twice the median value.

Quartile values close to the median will yield a deviation value near zero, while widely divergent quartile values will lead to a deviation value of one, or even higher. His results were as follows:

Table 2

The Unweighted Arithmetic Mean Tariff and Deviation from the Median of all Pre-EEC National Tariff Positions, 1955 [7]

Country	Unweighted Arithmetic Mean Tariff [8]	Interquartile Range Divided by Median [9]
Belgium-Luxembourg	9.5	0.93
France	18.1	0.38
Germany	15.5	0.54
Italy	17.3	0.35
Netherlands	9.5	0.93

The relatively high deviation of the Benelux tariffs indicates that the low-tariff Benelux countries retained a number of relatively high tariffs among their generally low duties. This means that, while it is true that these countries have been less protectionist than their EEC partners with respect to all imports, they retained significant tariff protection on certain import categories. The low countries produce almost no raw materials and are additionally dependent upon imports for a wide range of manufactured goods which likewise are not produced domestically; hence the large number of low duties. The relatively small number of goods which are produced domestically, in contrast, have received considerable tariff protection. This accounts for low unweighted mean tariff levels with fairly high deviations. By way of contrast, France and Italy imposed fairly high tariffs over a much wider variety of imports, thus leading to relatively high mean tariff values and fairly low deviations. The German case falls between the two extremes, with moderate values both for the mean tariff and the deviation about the median. [10]

The distribution of the relatively high mean tariff countries, France and Italy, approximates a fairly narrow normal curve around the 16-20 per cent tariff levels. The Belgium-Luxembourg distribution, with a relatively low mean tariff, is skewed to the right, demonstrating a large number of very low tariffs combined with a small, but significant, number of fairly high duties as well. The Dutch tariff distribution approximates that of the BLEU, while the German distribution falls between those of France and Italy on the one hand, and the BLEU on the other.

If the highly skewed BLEU distribution of tariffs on all imports is indicative of a relatively small number of high tariffs on certain manufactured imports combined with a large number of low tariffs on agricultural and raw materials imports, then the distribution of tariffs on industrial imports _alone_ should appear quite different. This is, in fact, the case. The modal tariff range here is 4-8 per cent instead of 0-4 per cent for _all_ imports, and a greater percentage of the duties is distributed in the higher tariff ranges. Similar comments could be made for the Dutch case. In contrast, the French and Italian distribution of tariffs on industrial imports closely corresponds to the respective distributions of tariffs on _all_ imports. In each case, the modal duty range is 16-20 per cent, but a greater percentage of the duties on industrial imports is found in the low-tariff portion of the distributions than is the case in the frequency distribution for _all_ imports. Again, Germany falls somewhere between the BLEU and French-Italian cases.

The general conclusions which may be drawn from these data center around the notion that, as regards trade in _manufactured_ goods, which comprises most of intra-EEC trade, the unweighted mean of all national tariff positions should not be taken categorically as an indication of the degree of protection accorded domestic producers or the degree of restriction of imports. While it is still true that the structure of pre-EEC Benelux duties on manufactures was, on the whole, significantly lower than that of France and Italy, this difference was not quite as great as indicated by a comparison of the unweighted means. Hence the expected growth of Benelux imports from EEC partner countries as a result of the gradual elimination of intra-EEC duties, relative to that occurring in the other three member countries, would be somewhat greater than that anticipated from an inspection and comparison of the unweighted means of all tariffs alone.

The following table compares the unweighted mean tariffs on all imports and manufactured imports, respectively, with the median tariff on manufactured imports:

Table 3

Comparison of Unweighted Mean and Median Pre-EEC Tariffs on All Imports and Manufactured Imports, 1955 [11] (expressed in per cent, ad valorem)

Country	Mean Duty on All Imports	Mean Duty on Manufactured Imports	Difference	Median Duty on Manufactured Imports
Belgium-Luxembourg	9.5	10.9	1.4	8.0
France	18.1	18.5	0.4	19.0
Germany	15.5	13.5	- 2.0	12.0
Italy	17.3	18.5	1.2	18.0
Netherlands	9.5	10.8	1.9	8.0

This illustrates that the tariff structures of the so-called low-tariff countries, Belgium-Luxembourg and the Netherlands, in 1955 retained a number of fairly high duties on manufactured imports, so that their respective mean tariffs on manufactures were slightly higher than the corresponding mean duties on all goods. Although the unweighted mean duties on manufactures of the low-tariff countries were still considerably lower than those of the high-tariff nations, the difference is no longer quite as great as indicated by a comparison of the respective unweighted mean duties on all imports.

Thus far, we have dealt with tariffs primarily with respect to their use in protecting domestic suppliers from foreign competition. While this is undoubtedly the most important application of this instrument of commercial policy, tariffs are also employed specifically for the purpose of raising fiscal revenues--in the form of so-called revenue tariffs. Since the goal of these levies is maximum revenue yield, they are imposed under circumstances which seem to justify an analysis of these duties apart from that of protective tariffs in general. Similarly, the removal of revenue tariffs within the over-all framework of the Common Market presents certain special problems, which are covered below.

REVENUE TARIFFS

It is well known that, apart from the protection accorded domestic producers by tariffs from import competition, customs duties also are an important source of revenue for the governments of many countries. Clearly, all tariffs yield fiscal revenues, if goods are imported under them, but certain duties are imposed solely for this particular purpose. Fortunately, it is not difficult to determine which tariffs are imposed for the purpose of yielding revenues, and which are intended primarily to protect domestic industry. Most prominently, duties levied on raw materials, tropical agricultural commodities, other products with low price elasticity of demand, and manufactures not produced at all domestically are generally imposed for fiscal reasons. The level of pre-EEC duties on such imports varied considerably from country to country.

For instance, whereas some countries imposed high tariffs on mineral fuels and by-products, others levied negligible duties on such imports: Benelux 3.1 per cent, France 6.8 per cent, Germany 49.7 per cent, and Italy 10.9 per cent.[12] Those revenues collected by German fiscal authorities by means of high duties on such relatively price-inelastic imports are collected by their Benelux counterparts by means of internal taxes of various types.

While this particular example may be somewhat extreme, similar instances may be cited in the case of revenue tariffs levied on imports of tobacco, alcoholic beverages, tropical fruits, coffee, tea, sugar, cocoa and, in the case of the Benelux countries, even automobiles. It should be clear that all of these goods are imported in considerable volume, generally are not supplied domestically, and face a relative price-inelastic domestic demand.

The gradual elimination of intra-EEC tariffs also involves the elimination of these national revenue duties on imports from partner countries, and the harmonization (imposition of a common external tariff) of revenue duties on imports from third countries. In the case of intra-EEC trade, this does not pose a troublesome problem since most imports subject to revenue duties do not enter into intra-community trade to any significant extent.[13] One notable exception is the Benelux revenue tariff on automobiles. While there is no question but that this tariff is scheduled to be eliminated in line with the general EEC internal tariff reduction program, it does pose a problem for the Benelux countries by necessitating a reallocation of the sources of government revenues. This is equally true in the gradual formation of EEC common external tariffs on imports from third countries usually subject to revenue duties. The high-tariff EEC member countries must adjust their revenue duties to the arithmetic average of all pre-EEC national tariffs on the commodity in question and find alternative sources for the replacement of the lost revenues.[14]

Revenue tariffs thus pose a relatively minor, though interesting, problem in intra-EEC trade liberalization, since they are mostly imposed on imports from non-member countries. We have seen that some problems will be encountered in reallocating government revenues lost both due to the gradual elimination of intra-EEC revenue tariffs which do exist, and due to the harmonization of external tariffs. As a special classification of trade restrictions they do not play a really significant role in an analysis of intra-community trade and hence need not be pursued at greater length here.

UNWEIGHTED VERSUS WEIGHTED MEAN TARIFFS

It was mentioned in Chapter 3 that the unweighted arithmetic mean of all national tariffs as an indicator of the protective, or restrictive, effect of the national tariff structure, even when combined, as above, with some measure of tariff dispersion about this mean, has occasionally been deemed insufficient for complete analysis of tariff restrictions. Ideally, of course, the restrictive effect of the tariff should be gauged by some measure of the value of the goods <u>not imported</u> under it, i.e., the difference between hypothetical imports in the absence of the tariff and actual imports. However, since it is hardly possible to get a meaningful estimate of the presumed imports without tariffs, it has been asserted that each tariff be weighted by the value of goods imported under it, and a weighted average taken of the results.[15] This notion was rejected earlier on theoretical grounds, and it remains here to investigate the practical problems involved in evaluating the usefulness of weighted averages.

The first two parts of this chapter have shown, on the basis of both the unweighted mean national tariffs and the accompanying dispersions, that before the institution of the EEC France and Italy possessed relatively restrictive tariffs, while the Benelux countries maintained more liberal tariff restrictions, with Germany falling somewhere in between. When the unweighted mean pre-EEC tariffs are compared with the corresponding weighted means, the following figures result:

Table 4

Comparison of Weighted and Unweighted Averages of Pre-EEC Import Tariffs, 1955 (per cent, *ad valorem*) [16]

Country	Unweighted Average	Weighted Average
Belgium - Luxembourg	9.5	4.3
Netherlands	9.5	5.5
Germany	15.5	5.6
Italy	17.3	7.1
France	18.1	5.1

The unweighted mean tariff of France is almost twice as high as that of the Netherlands, but the corresponding weighted means portray French tariffs as being actually *lower* than Dutch duties. Similarly, Italy has the highest weighted average duty but only the second highest unweighted mean tariff; additional comparisons of this sort may be made between the remaining EEC countries.

What accounts for this apparent discrepancy between weighted and unweighted averages of national tariff categories? Assume two countries, A and B, each import only two commodities, X and Y; and while both apply a 20 per cent *ad valorem* tariff on import X, country A imposes a prohibitive 80 per cent duty on good Y while country B applies only a 30 per cent duty on this latter import. The annual value A imports of good Y clearly would be minimal (say $100,000) while corresponding substantial imports of country B might be $40 million. We could thus develop the table presented in the appendix (Table 1).

Since almost no goods are imported into country A under its prohibitive tariff on commodity Y, the resulting weighted mean duty is lower than the corresponding duty for country B, which imposes a much less restrictive tariff on the same commodity. Thus a comparison between the weighted means of the tariff structures of the two countries presents a generally misleading impression of the comparative restrictiveness of their respective tariff structures, and of the degree of protection embodied in them. This general conclusion is applicable to the pre-EEC tariff structures of the Common Market countries, just as it applies to this greatly simplified example. Referring once more to Table 4, since France and Italy imported a minimal quantity of goods under their respective highly restrictive tariffs (hence the high unweighted mean tariff levels), most goods entered these countries under moderate or low duties, thus accounting for the low weighted figures. A similar comparison of pre-EEC weighted and unweighted mean tariff levels may be made for any two other Common Market countries and the same conclusion will be drawn. Unless a more appropriate system of weighting can be devised, the use of the unweighted mean tariff as a measure of the degree of restrictiveness of a given national tariff structure seems more justified, and has been generally adopted by the EEC authorities. The unweighted mean tariff, as shown earlier, may then be combined with an analysis of the degree of dispersion of national tariff positions, although the results seldom seem to be changed materially thereby in practice.

PRIMARY NON-TARIFF CONSIDERATIONS

It was indicated in Chapter 3, concerned with the *a priori* effects of intra-EEC tariff reductions, that non-tariff trade barriers can impede the expansion of intra-community trade and reallocation of production which would be expected to result on the basis of tariff removal alone. Quotas, turnover tax rebates and countervailing duties, customs formalities and pure food and drug regulations, packaging regulations, and the development of EEC-wide market-sharing cartels are examples in this category. Since this study is primarily concerned with developments during the 1958-65 period, the analysis of these factors is somewhat simplified. It is much more difficult to project the influence which such (often covert) trade-restricting factors as international cartels will have in the EEC in future years, especially in view of the powerful nature of these organizations in Western Europe in the past.

First, it was mentioned earlier that quotas have traditionally played a relatively minor role in impeding trade between the present six EEC member countries. Their primary application has been the limitation of agricultural commodity imports by the EEC nations from each other. One year after the inception of the Common Market in 1959, intra-EEC quotas were made non-discriminatory with respect to country of origin of the imports. Due to the limited use of quotas in intra-EEC trade, this action seems to have done little to disturb trade patterns.[17] All quotas on non-agricultural intra-community trade were eliminated at the end of 1961, by which time the quota system had been replaced by a complex "variable levy" system in the case of agricultural trade.[18] Again, the end of the quota system itself probably had relatively little influence on the total volume of intra-trade, due to the limited use of this means of trade restriction by the EEC countries. Isolated cases where the elimination of quotas did have a significant effect in increasing the volume of trade in specific commodities are presented in Chapter 6.

Perhaps a more important case of non-tariff trade restrictions involves the indirect tax systems of member countries. Although proposals were made during the 1958-63 period to substantially harmonize the indirect taxation systems of the respective EEC countries, generally by replacing turnover, sales, and excise taxes by value-added taxes wherever possible, these efforts did not bear fruit during these years. Thus the problems presented by the existence of varying turnover taxes to intra-EEC trade remained during the entire six-year period, just as it prevailed during the initial decade of the ECSC.[19]

Indirect taxes, under certain conditions, play an important role in trade by directly influencing international price competition. The most important of these indirect taxes in the EEC is the turnover tax, which most member countries employ as a prime source of tax revenues. In one form, this type of tax is imposed in a cumulative manner, at a relatively low rate, each time the goods change possession in the production-distribution cycle. Thus, the more times a good changes hands before the retail stage, the greater the total tax levied upon it. A second form of the turnover tax in the EEC is a 20-30 per cent levy imposed at the last stage of production or distribution on a value-added basis. The former is employed by all EEC countries except France, which uses the single-levy method.[20]

Turnover tax rates differ markedly from country to country, a fact which is complicated further by the exemption of all exporters in most EEC countries from the tax, usually through a turnover tax rebate. Thus manufacturers in a given EEC member country might have to pay a 4 per cent turnover tax if the output were sold domestically, but would not have to do so if it were sold abroad; hence the amount of revenue obtained from exports, *ceteris paribus*, would be greater than that realized from domestic sales by the amount of the turnover tax imposed on the particular firm's stage of production. On the surface, then, it would seem that the export price of a given good might be lower than the domestic price by the amount of the turnover tax, if the full burden of the tax is shifted forward to domestic purchasers, although this may not be the case in reality. In order to offset the exporting producer's exemption from his country's turnover tax, the importing country will impose a special levy, called a countervailing duty, on the good at the time it crosses the border. The level of this duty, designed to offset the exporter's exemption from his country's turnover tax, will generally be equal to the importing country's own turnover tax on the good involved.

Under conditions where both the exporting and importing countries use the multi-stage, cumulative turnover tax system, this situation could be depicted as follows:

Table 5

The Effect of Turnover Taxes, Rebates, and Countervailing Duties--Two-Country, One Commodity, Limited Case with Equal Production Costs

Coun-try	Pre-tax Sell-ing Price	Turn-over Tax	Domes-tic Sell-ing Price	Turn-over Tax Re-bate	Ex-port Price	For-eign Coun-ter-vailing Duty	For-eign Im-port Price
A	200	10%	220	20	200	20%	240
B	200	20%	240	40	200	10%	220

In this case, the mechanics are relatively simple. A's domestic selling price is 220 and all exports are given the 10 per cent turnover tax rebate. But A's exports at a price of 200 incur B's countervailing duty of 20 per cent, thereby bringing the foreign import price of its exports up to 240, exactly the domestic selling price of B's producers, including that country's turnover tax. A similar path is traced by B's exports to A, where the import price again equals the domestic producers' price, including the turnover tax. In such a case, the advantage gained by the exporter's exemption from his country's turnover tax is exactly offset by the importing country's countervailing duty.

More complex is the case where the basic prices in the two countries vary to some extent. Here the real economic advantage of producers in one country may well be effectively cancelled out by a high countervailing duty imposed on the part of the importing country.

Table 6

The Effect of Turnover Taxes, Rebates, and Countervailing Duties--Two-Country, One Commodity, Limited Case with Unequal Production Costs

Country	Pre-tax Selling Price	Turnover Tax	Domestic Selling Price	Turnover Tax Rebate	Export Price	Foreign Countervailing Duty	Foreign Import Price
A	200	5%	210	10	200	10%	220.0
B	150	10%	165	15	150	5%	157.5

The following relationships result:

Domestic production cost difference:
200(A) - 150(B) = 50
Domestic selling price difference:
210(A) - 165(B) = 45
Price difference of both sold in A:
210(A) - 157.5(B) = 52.5
Price difference of both sold in B:
220(A) - 165(B) = 55

Whereas the production cost difference is 50 in favor of B, the domestic selling price difference, after the turnover tax, is reduced to 45 in favor of B. However, when A exports to B its price disadvantage grows to 55; and when B exports to A its price advantage grows to 52.5. The implications of this sort of distortion of international price competition within the EEC are clear, even in the absence of tariffs or other barriers to trade.

This situation is further complicated by the fact that the countervailing duty imposed by the importing country is not necessarily always the same as its turnover tax, as the following table illustrates:

Table 7

Turnover Tax Exemptions and Countervailing Duties on Selected Raw Materials, 1953*

	Hard Coal		Coke		Billets		Hot-Drawn Plates	
	E	CD	E	CD	E	CD	E	CD
Germany	4	4	4	4	4	4	4	4
Belgium	4.5	4.5	1.75	4.5	4.5	4.5	4.5	4.5
France	7.35	8	7.35	8	8	20	16.35	20
Italy	-	3	-	3	3	3	3	3
Luxembourg	-	2	-	2	2	2	2	2
Netherlands	4	4	4	4	4	4	4	4

E = Turnover tax exemption.
CD = Countervailing duty.
*High Authority, European Coal and Steel Community, Report on the Problems Posed by the Turnover Tax to the Common Market (Luxembourg: High Authority, ECSC, 1953).

This results from the fact that the importing country must try to estimate the amount of tax from which the goods likely to be imported have been exempted. Since this would be impossible on the basis of every potential exporting country, the rates often must be more or less arbitrarily set. In addition, due to the fact that turnover tax exemptions, in the case of the multi-stage system, also often do not reflect the actual amount of tax resting on a product (which, of course, depends on the number of stages in the production cycle) the discrepancy between the turnover tax exemptions and countervailing duties of two countries can be considerable.

This is especially true in the case of trade between France and the remainder of the EEC. As has been mentioned earlier, France levies a value-added tax averaging 20 per cent on all goods, whose impact falls at the last stage, i.e., immediately before the good is transferred to the final consumer or user. The remaining member countries, on the other hand, impose a low tax cumulatively every time the good changes hands, which varies around 4 per cent and which, for a given product, may amount to as much as 15 per cent to 16 per cent, although for single-stage products it may be as low as 3 or 4 per cent.[21]

From the information presented, it should be clear that a given product traded between France and the remainder of the EEC will almost never incur a countervailing duty equal to its turnover tax exemption. That is, when a good is imported into France it will incur a countervailing duty of about 20 per cent, having perhaps exempted turnover taxes of only 3 to 5 per cent. Similarly, when the good is exported from France to one of the other EEC countries, it may have exempted a 20 per cent tax and will probably incur only a 2 to 5 per cent countervailing duty.

A simple example will serve to clarify the nature and extent of this distortion: Assume that a ton of aluminum ingot sells for $480.00 in country A, which uses a 4 per cent multi-stage cumulative turnover tax system. The same ton of aluminum costs $479.30 in country B, which employs a single-stage 20 per cent turnover levy. The difference is only $0.70. Both will impose countervailing duties on imports roughly equivalent to their own turnover taxes. Since aluminum production is a single-stage operation, when country A exports to country B, the aluminum will exempt a 4 per cent turnover tax and incur a 20 per cent countervailing duty. Similarly, when B ships aluminum to A, the aluminum will exempt a 20 per cent turnover tax and incur A's small 4 per cent countervailing duty. All this results in the fact that, while the domestic prices of the aluminum are roughly equivalent, A's aluminum sold in B will cost $552.96 per ton while B's aluminum exported to A will sell for a mere $398.78 the ton, for a difference of $154.18 per ton.

It is also apparent that goods with few stages of production will always have a competitive edge, when they are produced under the single-stage non-cumulative turnover tax system, over the same goods produced under the multi-stage, cumulative turnover tax system. Conversely, of course, goods requiring a relatively large number of stages of production will fare better if they are produced under the multi-stage system as compared with those produced in countries using the single-stage turnover tax structure.[22]

Finally, an example of such distortion of relative prices

may be taken from actual experience in the EEC.[23] In May of 1961 a ton of French steel rods cost $111.50 f.o.b. Thionville. At the same time, a ton of German steel rods cost $108.25 f.o.b. Oberhausen. Exports of the French steel to Germany can be calculated as follows:

	Basic price f.o.b. Thionville, France . . .	$111.50
less:	Turnover tax rebate at the French frontier	22.00
equals:	French export price	$ 89.50
plus:	German countervailing duty	5.00
	Freight charges Thionville-Oberhausen . .	6.25
equals:	Price of imported French steel in Oberhausen	$100.75

Conversely, the export of German steel to France may be shown as follows:

	Basic price f.o.b. Oberhausen	$108.25
less:	Turnover tax rebate at the German border	6.50
equals:	German export price	$101.75
plus:	French countervailing duty	25.50
	Freight charges Oberhausen-Thionville . .	6.25
equals:	Price of imported German steel in Thionville	$133.50

Here the price of French imported steel underbids German domestic steel despite the freight charges from Thionville to Oberhausen and despite the fact that the f.o.b. French price lies $3.25 over the German f.o.b. price.

The distortion of trade patterns and allocation of production based on production costs, due to differences in EEC turnover tax systems, remained in existence during the entire 1958-63 period under consideration here. Still, it is difficult to judge its effect in impeding the trade expansion which would normally be expected to result from the reduction of tariffs and other explicit trade barriers. It is clear that the influence of turnover taxes is of greatest significance in cases where the competing products are of fairly homogeneous quality and possess a high price elasticity of demand.[24]

As far as other non-tariff considerations are concerned, it is difficult to generalize as to their influence in impeding the trade growth that would otherwise result from the elimination of such, often covert, intra-EEC trade restrictions. Discriminatory freight rates, for instance, might serve to artificially enhance the competitiveness of certain industries, especially in less-developed regions such as the Italian Mezzogiorno, by lowering their freight charges on the government-owned railroads to the national customs frontier.[25] Other direct or indirect subsidies granted selected industries by the member governments could, and undoubtedly did, serve to impede the reallocation of production within the EEC purely according to production cost considerations. An analysis of these questions is outside the scope of this study and falls into the realm of Common Market competition and transport regulation, primarily governed by Articles 7 and 92 of the Treaty of Rome.[26]

Special charges and levies on imported goods may also be used to make it difficult or costly for purchasers in one member country to obtain goods from other EEC nations despite the existence of low and gradually declining import duties. For instance, fees and sales taxes have impeded the purchase of foreign automobiles in Italy, and extraordinarily high insurance premiums charged owners of imported automobiles in France are examples in this category.[27] Pressure exerted by the German brewing industry to have beer imports limited to that contained in German "standard" size and shape bottles is another case in point.[28] Foreign brewers would have to convert part or all production to bottles acceptable to the German authorities, thereby raising their costs and suffering in price competitiveness relative to German competitors. All such measures seek to continue protection of domestic production in the face of declining internal trade restrictions. Again, no general statements can be made, but these considerations will be taken into account in the analysis of intra-EEC trade growth of various manufactures in later chapters of this study.

Notes to Chapter 4

1. The question of weighted versus unweighted mean tariff levels is covered below.

2. Economist Intelligence Unit, "Tariffs on a Cross-Section of 28 Import Categories," Britain and Europe (London: EIU, 1957).

3. C.P. Kindleberger, International Economics,

(Homewood, Ill.: Richard D. Irwin, 1963), p. 155.

4. International Monetary Fund, _International Financial Statistics_ (Washington, D.C.: IMF, 1953, 1958).

5. A duty position may be defined as a relatively homogeneous group of goods to which a single tariff is applied, e.g., aircraft spares, metal furniture.

6. Binswanger, _op. cit._, 133-37.

7. _Ibid._, p. 134.

8. These unweighted mean tariffs do not coincide with those presented in Table 1 due to the different methods of calculation. Nevertheless, the rankings remain the same.

9. Deviations are computed by the method outlined in the text above.

10. See also Heinrich Megow, _Steuern und Zoelle im Gemeinsamen Markt_ (Baden-Baden: August Lutzeyer, 1962).

11. Binswanger, _op. cit._, pp. 134-38; for Netherlands, United Nations, Economic Commission for Europe, _Economic Survey of Europe - 1956_, "The Present Tariff Structure" (Geneva: U.N., 1957).

12. Committee for Economic Development, _European Tariffs and Trade_ (New York: CED, 1962).

13. See, for example, United Nations, Secretariat, Statistical Office, Statistical Papers Series D, _Commodity Trade Statistics_, various issues, 1955-65.

14. See Groeben and Boeckh, _op. cit._, _supra._

15. See Chapter 3.

16. Data compiled by Balassa, _op. cit._, p. 46. Weighted averages are computed by multiplying each tariff by the value of goods imported under it during a given year and dividing the result by the value weights (excludes revenue tariffs).

17. Whereas this may be true of trade in general, it may not hold for certain goods categories where quotas have played an important role.

18. An explanation of the agricultural developments in the EEC may be found in Uwe Kitzinger, The Politics and Economics of European Integration (New York: Praeger, 1964).

19. J.V. Wagenheim, "Der Einfluss der Steuern auf die Wettbewerbslage im gemeinsamen Stahlmarkt," Der Volkswirt (supplement), No. 46 (November 17, 1961).

20. See J. van Horn, "Das Problem der Harmonisierung der Steuern innerhalb der EWG," Deutsches Verwaltungsblatt, 1961, pp. 300-325.

21. G. Vedel, "Les Aspects Fiscaux du Marché Commun," Bulletin for Industrial Fiscal Documentation (Amsterdam), No. 12 (1960), p. 329.

22. See European Coal and Steel Community, Report on the Problems Posed by the Turnover Tax to the Common Market (Luxembourg: High Authority, ECSC, 1953).

23. Guenther Schmoelders, Steuerliche Wettbewerbsverzerrungen beim grenzueberschreitenden Warenverkehr im Gemeinsamen Markt (Cologne: Carl Heymanns Verlag), p. 30. (Values translated at $1.00: DM 4.00.)

24. See, in general, C. Cosciani, "Problèmes fiscaux de la Communauté Economique Européenne," Public Finance, Vol. VIII (1958), p. 197.

25. Whereas the harmonization of intra-EEC freight charges was foreseen in the Rome Treaty, there was little implementation of these provisions by the end of 1963. For an analysis of Common Market transport coordination and the progress achieved, see Finn B. Jensen and Ingo Walter, The Common Market: Economic Integration in Europe (Philadelphia: J.B. Lippincott Company, 1965), pp. 141-49.

26. A competent analysis of these problems may be found in M. Hochbaum, Das Diskriminierungs- und Subventionsverbot in der EGKS und EWG (Baden-Baden: August

Lutzeyer, 1962); see also Jensen and Walter, op. cit., pp. 132-41.

27. "Fragwuerdige EWG-Praxis," in Aussenhandel, April 9, 1964.

28. "Die deutschen Brauer wehren sich," Der Spiegel, November 15, 1964.

CHAPTER 5 GROWTH AND CHANGE IN THE DIRECTION OF EEC TRADE

The expected changes in the rate of growth of intra-area trade of the Common Market countries as well as the anticipated changes in the trade patterns of these countries in response to the formation of the EEC, based on the theory of economic integration, were presented in Chapter 3. It is necessary at this point to look at the facts: What happened to the EEC countries' trade in terms of growth and patterns during the post-EEC period under consideration? Moreover, is there any indication that such changes as did occur may in part be attributed to the gradual formation of an economic union, as outlined in Chapter 4?

In order to answer such questions, with respect to overall trade, we need to look at changes which occurred during the 1958-65 period in the direction of export and import flows both for the EEC as a whole and for the individual member countries. In addition, the rate of growth of intra-area trade during the post-EEC period should be compared to the corresponding pre-EEC growth rate, external trade growth, and the development of trade among other industrialized countries. Once this has been done, some statement may be possible as to the role of the EEC itself in influencing the trade patterns and growth of the participating countries.

GROWTH OF INTRA-EEC TRADE

According to the theoretical analysis presented earlier, it is clear that total trade among the EEC member nations should have grown more rapidly during the six years after the Common Market was formed, than during the six years prior to the creation of the EEC (under *ceteris paribus* conditions). It is equally clear that the EEC countries' total exports to the EEC should have grown more rapidly than exports to the rest of the world, and that total imports from the EEC should have grown more rapidly than imports from the rest of the world.

Moreover, if the theoretical evaluation, presented in Chapter 3, of both EEC and EFTA as economic integration projects is at all realistic, then the corresponding trade developments for EFTA should have been considerably less pronounced than for the Common Market. Finally, the above statements imply that the proportion of total trade carried on internally, on both the export and import side, should have grown for both the EEC and EFTA, but considerably more markedly in the case of the former.

Table 8

Growth of Intra-EEC Trade in Current and Constant Prices, 1953-65 [2]
(millions of U.S. dollars)

Years	Trade Volume Current Prices	Price Index	Trade Volume 1958 Prices	Average Annual Trade Growth Current Prices	Average Annual Trade Growth Constant Prices
1953	3936.7	98	4017.0		
1953-58				11.5%	11.1%
1958	6787.2	100	6787.2		
1958-63				18.3%	17.4%
1963	15720.0	104	15115.4		
1953-63				14.9%	14.3%
1958-65				16.6%	15.6%

It is evident from Table 8 that trade between the present member countries of the Common Market grew rapidly during the entire 1953-65 period: From 1953 to 1958 the average annual growth rate of intra-area trade for the EEC as a whole was 11.5 per cent, from 1958 to 1963 it was 18.3 per cent, and from 1958 to 1965 it was 16.6 per cent. These figures are based on data in current prices (Appendix Table 3). Although constant prices are necessary if we are interested the rates of growth themselves, current prices are adequate for comparison of the average annual rates of change over two or more periods of time as long as the average annual rates of change of the price levels did not vary materially from one period to the next. This condition is fulfilled in the case of the EEC, as seen in the Appendix, Tables 2 and 4, presenting movements in wholesale and export prices for each EEC country for 1953-58 and 1958-65. The relevant index of prices prevailing in intra-EEC trade is a weighted average of the export prices of each country.[1]

When these intra-EEC trade figures are deflated by the applicable price index, the average annual rate of intra-EEC trade growth for 1953-58 and 1958-63 was 11.1 per cent and 17.4 per cent, respectively, and 15.6 per cent for 1958-65.

It is evident that the difference between the average annual rates of trade growth of the periods before and after the establishment of the EEC was substantial, both in real and in current prices. We thus have a starting point for testing the hypothesis that economic integration had an expansionary effect on trade between the member countries. This would not be the case, however, if there were substantial evidence that the 1953-58 figure (11.5 per cent) was for some reason abnormally low. Fortunately, there is reason to believe that this figure is abnormally <u>high</u>. Continued trade and payments restrictions vis-a-vis the dollar-area countries during the last phase of the so-called dollar-shortage era tended to bias trade in the direction of the European countries. Hence, if there had been no discrimination during the 1953-58 period, in favor of non-dollar countries, one would expect the average annual rate of growth of intra-EEC trade to be somewhat lower than it actually was, and consequently there would have been an even more marked increase in the rate of intra-area trade growth from 1953-58 to 1958-65.

A second factor, to which we will return later, might also limit the responsibility of economic integration for this increase in the rate of trade growth. Trade varies with the level of GNP. Hence, if the rate of GNP growth of the EEC was substantially greater during 1958-65 than during 1953-58, at least part of the increased rate of growth of intra-area trade might be accounted for. However, as Table 9 shows, there is little evidence of acceleration in the rate of growth of the GNP of the Common Market countries: it was already very high during the last part of the Reconstruction era and the years immediately following (i.e., during the so-called catching up phase). In fact, the average annual rate of GNP growth, based on both the real and current prices, did not differ materially from 1958-65 to 1953-58.[3]

Table 9

Average Annual Rates of GNP Growth and Price Level Change, 1953-65 [5] (per cent per year)

Country	Average Annual Rates of GNP Growth						Average Annual Rates of Wholesale and Export Price Rise					
	1953-58		1958-63		1958-65		1953-58		1958-63		1958-65	
	Current	Real	Current	Real	Current	Real	Wholesale	Export	Wholesale	Export	Wholesale	Export
France	9.0	4.7	9.9	5.7	9.3	5.1	2.6	2.5	2.8	2.6	2.9	2.9
Germany	9.9	7.6	10.3	7.7	9.9	7.5	0.3	0.2	0.3	0.1	2.0	0.1
Italy	7.5	6.0	10.3	7.5	9.3	6.5	0.1	-0.9	0.3	-0.6	1.6	-0.4
Netherlands	5.3	5.7	7.8	5.3	9.0	6.2	0.2	-0.1	0.3	-0.6	1.4	0.1
Belg.-Lux.	8.1	3.5	4.7	3.2	5.3	3.3	0.2	0.1	0.1	-0.5	1.3	0.0
EEC*	9.1	5.4	9.7	6.3	9.4	6.1	0.9	1.4	1.0	0.6	2.0	0.8

* Weighted Averages: GNP and wholesale price figures weighted by the per cent of total EEC GNP contributed by each country. Export price figures weighted by the per cent of total EEC exports originating in each member country. Figures for 1958-65 are estimates.

A rather more subtle point may be made in this connection. Table 9 shows that the rate of GNP growth of the EEC was not much different during 1958-63 than during 1953-58, and hence could not itself have brought about an acceleration in intra-EEC trade growth. However, is it not possible that the EEC itself in fact caused the member countries GNP growth to be higher than it would have been in the absence of the community? That is, is it likely that the rate of growth of the Common Market real GNP during the 1958-63 period would have slowed to, say, 3.8 or 4.0 per cent per year if there had been no Common Market? One extensive study answers this question in the affirmative, giving the EEC a great deal of credit for maintaining a high rate of economic growth in the member countries.[4]

If this latter idea is given any weight at all, then the EEC may have been responsible for the rapid growth of trade among the participating countries in two ways: by helping to maintain a high rate of economic growth and by influencing the volume of trade directly through gradual elimination of protective barriers to internal trade.

A very preliminary conclusion, based on the above data, is that the EEC did in fact stimulate the growth of intra-area trade, although the magnitude of this stimulus is uncertain and subject to further study below. It is perhaps worthwhile to cite here a number of considerations which would seem to limit this initial conclusion. First, doubts have been expressed that the first two or three 10 per cent intra-EEC tariff reductions could have had much influence on the over-all volume of internal trade. Only those commodities having high price elasticity of demand could have been greatly affected by these initial reductions, and it is doubtful that these particular commodities comprised a sizable portion of overall trade volume. Second, the possibility of compensatory taxes and other changes offsetting the impact of tariff reductions was mentioned in Chapter 4, and this may have mitigated somewhat the trade-expansionary force of at least the first two or three 10 per cent tariff cuts. Third, the influence of the periodic 10 per cent tariff reductions throughout the 1958-65 period cannot be isolated very well, especially since Germany undertook significant reductions of tariffs on imports during 1957 for reasons not associated with the EEC.

Further complication for the analysis of the impact of the

EEC on internal trade growth arises out of changes which occurred in the values of the German mark, French franc, and Dutch guilder during and immediately prior to the 1958-65 period under consideration here. France devalued by 40 per cent in two stages in 1957 and 1958; Germany and the Netherlands undertook an upward revaluation of their respective currencies in 1961. Devaluation of the franc in 1957-58 presumably dampened French demand for imports from the EEC and stimulated demand for French exports on the part of the remaining EEC countries. Hence we would expect to see an increase in intra-EEC imports from France and a decline in French imports from the rest of the Common Market. The net effect, on the volume of intra-EEC trade, of the French devaluation constitutes a balance between these two expansionary and contractionary forces; its magnitude depends upon the relevant elasticities of demand for imports on the part of both France and the rest of the EEC. The same holds true, to a lesser extent and in an opposite manner, in the case of the German and Dutch upward revaluation.

The net effect of these changes on currency values on the part of France, the Netherlands, and Germany on intra-EEC trade would be difficult to determine precisely. To do so would require a knowledge of price elasticities of demand and supply for imports and exports, respectively, for these three countries as well as price elasticity of demand for imports of the remaining EEC nations. Import and export elasticities are extremely difficult, if not impossible, to isolate and any such figures derived would surely be little more than guesses. Tables 2 and 3 in the Appendix show that there was apparently little reaction in the value of intra-EEC imports or exports on the part of France after its devaluation and equally little indication of change in the intra-EEC trade of the Netherlands and Germany as a result of their respective upward revaluations.

Whereas it is certainly not justifiable to assert that changes in the values of EEC currencies had little or no effect on the over-all volume of intra-area trade, it seems safe to say that they were not of determining importance. Moreover, the significant French devaluation came almost a year before the first EEC tariff reductions took effect, while the magnitude of the Dutch and German revaluations was small. While they undoubtedly did influence the direction of intra-EEC trade to some degree, there is little evidence supporting a decisive influence on the over-all volume of trade among the Common Market member nations.

A final question which has been raised relates to the extension of several of the reductions in intra-EEC trade barriers to non-member countries as well. Notable are the first 10 per cent tariff cut in 1959, which was extended to all non-member countries as well, the reduction of trade barriers vis-a-vis the underdeveloped countries associated with the EEC and, finally, the numerous trade agreements reached between the EEC and third countries during the 1958-65 period.

Opposing these notions that the EEC really could not have had a substantial stimulative effect during the period under consideration is another, rather intangible, idea: namely, the force of expectations.

As early as 1958, it was widely believed among EEC businessmen that the Common Market tariff removal program would eventually be brought to a successful conclusion. Such expectations could easily have led to an increase in the rate of trade growth among EEC nations even without the actual tariff cuts, i.e., in anticipation of their impending implementation.[6]

This notion is reinforced by the apparent actions of U.S. businessmen operating plants in the EEC area. For instance, one U.S. firm had several plants in the Common Market, each of which produced a full line of heavy capital equipment for the national market until 1959. Thereafter, in anticipation of the completion of the customs union, each plant was made to specialize in a more limited range of output, thereby realizing significant internal economies and serving the entire EEC area. This specialization of production was undertaken largely in anticipation of economic integration and despite initial losses due to the incomplete removal of intra-EEC customs duties. If such action was widespread on the part of Common Market firms, the "anticipation effect" could have been powerful indeed.

Since it would be clearly impossible to separate the influence of anticipations, changes in currency values, compensation tariffs, pre-EEC tariff reductions, and Common Market trade liberalization with respect to non-member countries, on the volume of intra-EEC trade or on its rate of growth, it is questionable whether a more detailed attempt at such an analysis, undoubtedly ending in speculation, would contribute significantly to this study.

We may, however, break down intra-EEC trade growth by the participating countries to see whether there was any relation between it and the extent of reductions in trade barriers.

Table 10

Changes in Tariffs and Rates of Import Growth, 1953-65 (in real terms) [7]

Country	Average Annual Growth of Intra-EEC Imports (per cent)*			Relative Increase from Period 1 to Period 2	Relative Increase from Period 1 to Period 3	1958-65 Tariff Decline, Rank
	(1) 1953-58	(2) 1958-63	(3) 1958-65			
France	14.6	21.0	17.2	44%	18%	2
Germany	15.3	16.4	18.7	7%	22%	3
Italy	3.9	28.2	16.6	623%	326%	1
Netherlands	6.7	14.3	13.0	113%	94%	4
Belgium-Lux.	8.9	11.9	11.3	34%	27%	5
EEC	11.1	17.4	15.6	57%	41%	-

* Based on trade figures deflated by the weighted average of export prices of the EEC partners for each member country. Data for 1958-65 are estimates.

Most striking is the case of Italy, with a more than sixfold increase in the rate of intra-area import growth. This may be partly explained by acceleration of the rate of growth of Italian GNP during the post-EEC period, which was more substantial than that of the other EEC countries (see Appendix Table 7). As mentioned earlier in a more general context, part of this rapid growth of Italian GNP during the 1958-63 period was undoubtedly also associated with the EEC by being partly export-led and hence itself stimulated to some extent by the Common Market. The rate of growth of Italian imports from non-member countries during 1958-63 was significantly lower (8.9 per cent vs. 28.2 per cent) despite the fact that both should have been affected equally by GNP growth, and that Italian duties on imports from third countries declined in accordance with the adjustment to the EEC common external tariff (see Appendix Table 3).

On the whole, Table 11 does not present much evidence to conclude that the reduction of intra-EEC tariffs was the primary factor responsible for the increase in the rate of intra-EEC trade growth which we know occurred.

On the other hand, if it is asserted that the tariff effect should have borne on the rates of trade growth themselves, rather than on the change in the rates of trade growth between the pre-EEC and post-EEC periods, the results of a rank correlation analysis for 1958-63 seem much more convincing.

Table 11

Intra-EEC Tariff Reductions and Trade Growth, 1958-63[8]

Country	Internal Tariff Decline* from	to	Rank	Average Annual Rate of Trade Growth**	Rank
Italy	25.5	10.2	1	28.2	1
France	24.0	9.6	2	21.0	2
Germany	10.0	4.0	3	16.4	3
Netherlands	9.2	3.8	4	14.3	4
Belg.-Lux.	8.8	3.4	5	11.9	5

* Tariffs expressed in per cent *ad valorem*, on a cross-section of 28 import categories as compiled by the Economist Intelligence Unit.

** Based on trade data in constant prices.

In this case, the coefficient of rank correlation is, of course, 1.00. If, as has been asserted earlier, a large number of special factors influenced the rate of intra-EEC trade growth, both before and after 1958, then perhaps the rates of growth themselves are significant, and not the change in those rates of growth from one period to the next. If such is the case, the results of the analysis of trade growth lend much more support for the *a priori* statements based on the theory of economic integration.

SHIFTS IN THE DIRECTION OF TRADE

If the theoretical indications as to changes in the direction of trade of the Common Market countries is to be supported by the facts, then we would expect to find an increasing share of the exports of each of the EEC countries being directed to its partners subsequent to the formation of the community in 1958. Similarly, an increasing percentage of total imports of each member country should be accounted for by the EEC in response to tariff removal, expectations, and other factors associated with the Common Market.

In short, each EEC country should draw more of its imports from, and send more of its exports to, the rest of the Common Market in 1963 and 1965 than in 1958. If there is any reason to suspect that such increasing "regionalization" of trade would have occurred anyway, even in the absence of the EEC, this would be expected to show up in the 1953-58 data as well. The presence of any significant acceleration in the trend toward regionalization of trade from 1953-58 to 1958-63 or 1958-65 could then, in part, be ascribed to the formation of the Common Market.

In 1953, 28.4 per cent of total EEC exports were destined for the EEC. This figure showed no real trend during the 1953-58 period, and in 1958 stood at 30.8 per cent (see Appendix Table 9). Thereafter it rose rapidly every year until in 1963 42.4 per cent of total EEC exports went to the EEC (approximately 43.4 per cent in 1965). On the import side, the changes are less pronounced but still significant. In 1953, 26.3 per cent of total EEC imports came from the EEC, which rose slowly to 29.6 per cent in 1958. Thereafter the regionalization of imports became more pronounced, and by 1963 38.9 per cent of total EEC imports originated in the EEC (41.6 per cent in 1965). The complete data on the direction of trade of the Common Market countries is presented in the Appendix Table 9 and summarized in Table 12.

In 1958, at the outset of the EEC, Belgium-Luxembourg sold 58.4 per cent of its exports in non-EEC countries, with only 41.6 per cent going to its Common Market partners. By the end of 1963, however, this relationship had been reversed with 60.7 per cent of BLEU exports going to the remainder of the EEC and only 39.3 per cent destined for third countries. This was even more pronounced in 1965. During the post-EEC period, then, the Common Market had replaced the rest of the world as the prime market for BLEU exports. To a lesser degree, the same shift in the quantitative importance of export markets occurred in the Netherlands over the same time span. Whereas 42.7 per cent of Dutch exports in 1958 was destined for the Common Market members, this figure had risen to 53.4 per cent in 1963 and 55.5 per cent in 1965. Since the smaller EEC countries--Belgium, Luxembourg, and the Netherlands--have become most dependent upon the EEC as a market for their export, they had a great deal to lose if the EEC were to fail and trade restrictions were reimposed. This probably accounts at least partly for the intense interest which these countries have displayed in the success of the Common Market since its inception. Although for the Benelux countries alone the EEC became the primary market for exports during 1958-65 (i.e., over 50 per cent of total exports), the importance of the EEC as a market for the exports of each of the remaining member countries also increased respectably during this period.

While it is clear that the shift in the direction of trade has been in favor of the EEC in the case of each member country, this shift was considerably more pronounced during 1958-65 than during the 1953-58 pre-EEC period. The tendency toward regionalization of exports seems to have been present even before the EEC, especially in the case of the Netherlands and Italy.

The Dutch case probably reflected rapid expansion of intra-Benelux trade, as evidenced by the corresponding Belgium-Luxembourg import figures. The Italian case may reflect some "catching up" in the late reconstruction period, plus rapid growth of demand for subtropical and tropical agricultural commodities in the rest of the member countries.

Table 12

Change in the Direction of EEC Trade, 1953-65 [9]

Country	Per cent of Total Exports Going to EEC				Per cent of Total Imports Coming from EEC				Change in Direction of Exports [10]			Change in Direction of Imports [10]		
	1953	1958	1963	1965	1953	1958	1963	1965	'53-'58	'58-'63	'58-'65	'53-'58	'58-'63	'58-'65
France	19.7	22.0	37.5	40.9	16.3	21.9	35.7	38.8	+2.3	+15.5	+18.9	+5.6	+13.8	+16.9
Germany	29.8	27.2	37.3	35.2	25.1	25.6	33.3	37.8	-2.6	+10.1	+ 8.0	+0.4	+ 7.7	+12.2
Italy	20.6	26.5	35.5	40.2	22.0	21.6	32.8	31.2	+5.9	+ 9.0	+13.7	-0.4	+11.2	+ 9.6
Netherlands	35.6	42.7	53.4	55.7	36.8	41.9	51.6	53.4	+7.1	+10.7	+13.0	+5.1	+ 9.7	+11.5
Belg.-Lux.	38.4	41.6	60.7	62.0	38.6	46.6	52.6	54.5	+3.2	+19.1	+20.4	+8.0	+ 6.0	+ 7.9
All-EEC	28.4	30.5	42.4	43.5	26.3	29.6	38.9	41.6	+2.1	+11.9	+13.0	+3.3	+ 9.3	+12.0

Nevertheless, in each and every case, the tendency toward regionalization was far more pronounced during the post-EEC period. Regionalization of exports may be more indicative of the effect of the removal of intra-EEC trade barriers, or the anticipation thereof, since the problem of EEC tariff discrimination against third countries does not arise.

For this reason, it is surprising to find regionalization of imports during the post-EEC period to be less pronounced than regionalization of exports. In fact, there was a greater tendency toward regionalization of imports than exports prior to the advent of the EEC, and a lesser tendency afterward. This seems to refute the often-repeated charge of EEC trade discrimination against suppliers in third countries.

If there was in fact a tendency for increasing concentration on intra-trade before the EEC, then we would not be unjustified in saying that the regionalization of trade of the Common Market countries is at least partially a function of time. This has been brought out in a very comprehensive econometric study by Thorbecke with respect to all the world's industrialized countries.[11] A historic tendency for increasing concentration on EEC intra-trade would help explain part of the regionalization which we know occurred after the EEC was formed.

For an analysis of this question, we may use the following relation:[12]

$$\frac{X_{t+5}^{eec}}{X_{t+5}^{w}} = \frac{X_t^{eec}}{X_t^{w}} (1 + \underline{a})^5$$

where: X^{eec} = total EEC exports to the EEC
X^{w} = total EEC exports
t = base year (i. e., 1953 and 1958)
$t+5$ = terminal year (i. e., 1958 and 1963)
$\underline{a}$ = average annual rate of movement toward regionalization of imports.

If there were no tendency toward rationalization of trade prior to the EEC, a would be zero for the 1953-58 period. On the other hand, if a is positive for 1953-58, it may be compared with the corresponding value of a for the post-EEC 1958-63 period. The same procedure may be used in the case of imports, that is:

$$\frac{M_{t+5}^{eec}}{M_{t+5}^{w}} = \frac{M_{t}^{eec}}{M_{t}^{w}} (1 + \underline{b})^5$$

where: M^{eec} = total EEC imports from the EEC
M^{w} = total EEC imports
t = base year (i.e., 1953 and 1958)
$t+5$ = terminal year (i.e., 1958 and 1963)
$\underline{b}$ = average annual rate of regionalization of imports.

Computing the values for a (rate of regionalization of exports) and b (rate of regionalization of imports) confirms the findings presented earlier. There was a tendency for regionalization of exports among the EEC countries even before the Common Market, but this tendency grew far more pronounced after 1958. On the other hand, the corresponding acceleration of regionalization of imports was not as great as in the case of exports, as the following table shows:

Table 13

Rate of Regionalization of Common Market Trade, 1953-63[13] (in per cent per annum)

	1953-58	1958-63	Difference
Imports (b)*	2.18	5.63	+3.45
Exports (a)	1.45	6.82	+5.37

* Calculation of the values for a and b are explained in the text above and represent the average annual rate of increase in the importance of intra-area trade relative to total trade.

It is clear that the tendency for regionalization of Common Market trade, on both the export and the import side, was far more pronounced in the post-EEC period than during the years immediately prior to the establishment of the Common Market. Although this conclusion must be modified to some degree due to peculiarities in the base and terminal years chosen, there is little question but that it still applies. Since there is little reason for believing that the rate of regionalization should normally have been greater in the post-EEC period than before (in fact, it should actually be less, due to the liberalization of trade with respect to the dollar area), we may conclude that formation of the Common Market must have had a great deal to do with it.

The same procedure may be employed with respect to each of the EEC countries, and the results are summarized below:

Table 14

Rate of Regionalization of Trade of Individual EEC Countries, 1953-1963 [14]
(in per cent per annum)

Country	Imports		Exports	
	1953-58	1958-63	1953-58	1958-63
France	6.1	10.3	2.3	11.3
Germany	0.4	5.4	-0.8	6.5
Italy	-0.9	8.7	5.2	6.0
Netherlands	2.5	4.3	3.7	4.6
Belgium-Luxembourg	3.7	2.5	1.6	7.8

It is clear from these data that the rate of regionalization of exports rose for EEC member countries from one period to the next. This was most apparent in the case of Belgium-Luxembourg and France, and least so in the case of the Netherlands. The rate of regionalization of imports likewise increased from 1953-58 to 1958-63 for all countries except Belgium-Luxembourg, but less markedly than in the case of exports. The Belgium-Luxembourg data actually evidence a decline in the rate of regionalization of imports, possibly because the 1953-58 rate was already very high due to intra-Benelux trade growth, which was in excess of the growth of Belgium-Luxembourg trade with the rest of the EEC and with the rest of the world.

The question of distortion of the 1953-58 trade

regionalization figures by dollar-shortage considerations, already mentioned in connection with total EEC trade growth, also applies in this case. The 1953-58 regionalization figures presented here should be abnormally high for imports and low for exports, since the EEC countries during that period still discriminated against dollar goods and strove to export as much as possible to the dollar area.

Having looked at the regionalization of exports and imports separately, it is now advisable to integrate the two in order to see what happened to the direction of total EEC trade.

The primary shortcoming of the above analysis is that it is not able to bring out the "EEC effect" in any really quantifiable way. It is clear that the rate of regionalization of both imports and exports increased greatly after the formation of the EEC, but much more strikingly in the case of exports. This is partly due to the various factors which affect import and export shares. Change in the percentage of EEC exports destined for the EEC depends on GNP growth in the EEC relative to GNP growth in the rest of the world, as well as changes in trade restrictions in both the EEC and the rest of the world. Change in the percentage of EEC imports originating in the EEC, on the other hand, depends primarily on changes in EEC internal and external trade barriers, and supply conditions in the EEC and the rest of the world. Expectations and elasticities of demand for imports affect the regionalization of both EEC imports and exports.

The regionalization of over-all trade can be determined by looking at the regionalization, or movement in share indexes, of both imports and exports via a weighted arithmetic mean of the pre-EEC and post-EEC import and export shares. If we let both i and j stand for the EEC, the weighted share index of total intra-EEC trade (Aij) can be computed as follows: [15]

$$A_{ij} = \frac{X_{ij}\,(2-\mu_{ij}-\beta_{ij})}{(1-\beta_{ij})\,M_i + (1-\mu_{ij})\,N_j} \times 100$$

where: μ_{ij} = the initial import-share of j in i

β_{ij} = the initial export-share of i in j's total exports

M_i = index of i's total imports

N_j = index of j's total exports

X_{ij} = index of total intra-EEC trade.

Two weighted share indexes, one of 1958 with respect to the base year 1953 and the second for 1963 with respect to the base year 1958 (i.e., for the pre-EEC and post-EEC five-year periods) are 105 and 135, representing an increase of 28.6 per cent.

From the above formula, it is clear that the possibility of an increasing share index is less, the larger the export and import shares in the base year. Under "normal" conditions it should take a value of around 100, and significant departures from this figure can be attributed to changes in tariff barriers, changes in tastes, expectations, and so forth.[16] If the authors of the above-cited study are correct, then the higher 1958-63 figure should signify a relatively high "EEC-effect," specifically, 28.6 per cent of the weighted share. This, of course, tends to corroborate the results of the earlier analysis of trade within the Common Market.

This conclusion will be reinforced if it is found that there is a high degree of correspondence between the respective weighted share indexes and the tariff reductions for intra-EEC imports of the six member countries. These data are presented in Table 15 below and may be compared with the corresponding tariff reductions presented in Table 11.

Table 15

Weighted Share Indexes for 1963 (1958=100), Total Trade[17]

Importing Countries	Exporting Countries: France	Germany	Italy	Netherlands	Belgium-Luxembourg	EEC
France	-	135	172	153	128	147
Germany	198	-	178	140	130	156
Italy	192	121	-	156	132	136
Netherlands	132	105	171	-	103	108
Belg.-Lux.	131	102	153	105	-	127
EEC	172	107	168	132	112	135

It is clear that trade among the Benelux countries has not been affected greatly by the Common Market, since the weighted share indexes are close to 100 in each case. Because Benelux tariffs were already low at the inception of the Common Market, the German weighted share index in both the Netherlands and Belgium-Luxembourg is very low: 105 and 102, respectively. The corresponding French and Italian weighted share indexes are high, despite the very moderate decline in internal tariffs, primarily due to their extremely low initial import shares in the Benelux countries. Here, too, expectations and other intangible factors associated with the EEC could partially explain the high French and Italian weighted share indexes.

According to our expectations, the weighted share indexes of mutual trade among the three high-tariff countries--Italy, France, and Germany--are in fact very high. Similarly, the weighted share indexes of the Benelux in these high-tariff countries are also high, hence supporting the initial contention that there should be a fairly good rank correlation between the weighted import-share indexes and the level of initial national tariffs.

Thus far, we have looked at changes in the rate of intra-EEC trade growth, shifts in the direction of trade, and movements in the weighted share indexes of intra-EEC trade. Each method of analysis suggests that the Common Market must have had a great deal to do with the changes in the rate of trade growth and in the direction of trade which we know occurred.

THE ROLE OF INCOME CHANGES

To summarize, we know that a variety of factors affected the volume of intra-EEC trade during the 1958-65, post-Common Market period. Among these are changes in tastes (q), change in the real incomes of the member countries (y), change in intra-EEC tariffs and other trade restrictions (n), anticipations (x), economic policy considerations (p), time (t), and other factors represented by a residual (r). Hence we can incorporate the factors affecting the rate of intra-EEC trade growth from 1958 to 1965 (w) in a relation such as the following, where a, b, c, d, e, and f are weights attached to each of the factors:

$$w = an + bp + cx + dq + et + fy + r$$

It can be argued that the first four factors as well as the residual were profoundly affected by the Common Market. Tariff removal, anticipations, and government policy considerations are obvious ones, and have been argued earlier. Less obvious is the effect of the Common Market on changes in tastes in the member countries, which in turn may have helped to bring about increased intra-trade. This, too, has been argued in Chapter 3 and a good case can be made for the statement that economic integration affects tastes in such a way as to make them less of an obstacle to, and even an agent promoting, the expansion of trade within the integrating area. We have also analyzed the time element above and, although there was some tendency for increasing regionalization of the trade of the Common Market countries even before the EEC was formed, very little of the actual post-EEC trade regionalization can be explained by it. The residual itself may have reflected a good deal of the impact of the Common Market. For example, the EEC promoted labor migration, capital mobility, community-wide integration of firms and integrated transport, and each of these factors could have had a considerable impact on intra-area trade growth.

We are left, then, with income as being the one remaining variable which might to some extent explain the rapid growth of intra-EEC trade, although even income is hardly independent of the forces accompanying economic integration. Assuming for the moment that real GNP of the EEC member countries was, in fact, unaffected by the formation of the Common Market during the post-EEC period, the separate impact of GNP growth on intra-EEC trade can be at least roughly determined.

This may be done by means of a partial average propensity to import, applying only to the imports of each of the EEC member countries from the EEC. This "average regional propensity to import" may be defined in the case of any single member country as total real imports from the EEC divided by real GNP. Table 16 presents the average regional propensity to import for each EEC country during the pre-EEC 1953-58 period.

These propensities are calculated by dividing intra-EEC imports, deflated by an appropriate price index (see Appendix Table 4), by GNP, deflated by the GNP price index (Appendix Table 6).

Table 16

Average Propensities to Import from EEC, 1953-57 and Projected 1963 [18]
(in per cent)

Year	France	Germany	Italy	Netherlands	Belgium-Luxembourg
1953	1.5	2.8	3.0	14.2	10.8
1954	1.6	3.2	3.3	16.6	11.9
1955	2.0	3.8	3.3	18.7	11.9
1956	2.4	3.7	3.3	20.7	14.7
1957	2.6	3.7	3.4	21.3	15.1
I: 1963*	2.3	3.7	3.3	20.2	13.9
II:1963*	3.8	3.7	3.3	25.9	19.5

* I and II denote computation of anticipated 1963 average regional propensity to import under assumptions I and II, respectively, presented in the text below.

In the absence of the EEC, there is little reason to expect the average regional propensities to import to vary over the 1958-63 period with respect to what they were in 1953-57. Hence we can calculate what the volume of intra-EEC trade in 1963 should have been, based on the member countries' real GNP of that year and on the values of their respective regional propensities to import prior to the formation of the EEC. Here we will make two alternative assumptions, leading to different values for the hypothetical volume of 1963 intra-EEC trade:

Assumption I: The average regional propensity to import in 1963 of each EEC member country is the arithmetic mean of the corresponding values for the three years immediately preceding the formation of the EEC, i.e., 1955, 1956, and 1957.

Assumption II: If there is any marked trend in the average regional propensity to import during the pre-EEC period, the trend is extrapolated to 1963, and the corresponding figure for 1963 determined in this manner.

The 1963 calculated average regional propensities to import, under the two different assumptions, are given in the last two rows of Table 16 above. It is clear that the 1963 figure under Assumption II, in the case of France, the Netherlands, and Belgium-Luxembourg, is larger than the corresponding figure under Assumption I. Moreover, the former can be considered to be maximal, since there is little reason why the average regional propensity to import should continue to rise in the absence of some integrating force such as the Common Market.

Using the figures for the average regional propensities to import of the EEC member nations, derived above, the hypothetical intra-EEC imports of each country can be calculated for 1963 under both Assumption I and II. This is done in Table 17.

Table 17

Calculated and Actual 1963 Intra-EEC Imports (millions of U.S. dollars at 1958 prices)[19]

Country	(1) 1963 Calculated Imports (Assumption I)	(2) 1963 Calculated Imports (Assumption II)	(3) 1963 Actual Imports	(4) % of* Actual Attributed to EEC (Assumption I)	(5) % of** Actual Attributed to EEC (Assumption II)
France	1,208.88	1,997.28	3,183.67	62.0	37.3
Germany	2,758.72	2,758.72	4,298.61	35.8	35.8
Italy	1,157.64	1,157.64	2,416.31	52.1	52.1
Netherlands	2,167.46	2,775.07	2,991.84	27.6	7.1
Belg.-Lux.	1,588.77	2,228.85	2,609.70	39.1	14.6
Total EEC	8,865.60	10,895.34	15,500.13	42.8	29.7

* Column 3 less column 1 divided by column 3 times 100.
**Column 3 less column 2 divided by column 3 times 100.

It is clear that all of the calculated 1963 trade volumes are well below the actual figure. Columns 4 and 5 present the percentage of the actual 1963 trade volume which may be attributed to the EEC under the two differing assumptions. If the regional import propensities remained constant, then 42.8 per cent of total 1963 intra-EEC trade was attributable to the Common Market, i.e., without the EEC it would have been that much lower. Under Assumption II, the per cent of 1963 intra-area trade attributable to the EEC drops to 29.7 per cent.

At first glance, all of these figures may seem to be unreasonably high. However, in view of the pervasive influence of the EEC on so many of the factors affecting the volume of intra-EEC trade--including GNP growth--they do not seem out of the question after all. Moreover, these figures are less surprising when viewed in the light of the results obtained by the earlier methods of analysis in this chapter.

Once again, it is clear that those countries with the highest pre-EEC trade barriers apparently reacted most to the formation of the Common Market: Italy and France. This is true under both Assumptions I and II. Similarly, the countries which reacted least were those with the lowest initial tariff barriers: the Netherlands and Belgium-Luxembourg. These data, when combined with the foregoing analyses, present substantial evidence in support of the influence of the EEC on trade among the member countries, in spite of the fact that no numerical value can be assigned to this factor.

THE ROLE OF PRICE CHANGES

Although the discussion thus far has not considered explicitly any sort of price effects, there are three kinds of price effects which could have had a substantial impact on intra-EEC trade: price changes due to internal tariff reduction, currency revaluation, and differential rates of price level change. All three are difficult to get at directly due to the near-impossibility of measuring the price elasticity of demand for broad groups of goods, let alone all traded goods combined. Hence we have included price effects due to intra-EEC tariff reductions in our estimation of the over-all "EEC effect"; there is little reason to attempt to isolate or separate the tariff effect for purposes of the present study.

Another kind of price effect which certainly must have influenced the volume of intra-EEC trade to some degree is the role of increases in the domestic price level which took place in a given EEC member country, relative to the rates of price level rise which occurred in other Common Market nations, during the 1958-65 period. Relatively rising prices make domestically produced goods less competitive both at home and in export markets, and tend to reduce the value of exports and increase imports, especially in view of progressively decreasing trade restrictions on imports from EEC partner countries. Again, the nature of the relationship between a rise in the domestic price level and increases in the value of imports from Common Market partner countries is difficult to pin down in any really meaningful way. This is because so many other factors influence the volume of imports and because domestic inflation may be induced in part by a strong export-demand pull from other EEC nations.[20]

An analysis of changing relative price levels in the EEC is presented in the Appendix, Tables 4, 5, and 6.

According to these data, rapidly rising domestic prices could have had the effect of stimulating imports to any significant degree, primarily in the case of France. The French wholesale price index rose rapidly during the post-EEC 1958-63 period. At the same time, the wholesale price indexes of all other Common Market countries show only slight increases since 1953, and the Belgium-Luxembourg and Netherlands data even show some wholesale price declines since 1957. France alone could thus have undergone a substantial expansion of imports from EEC partner countries attributable to rising domestic prices between 1957 and 1963, based on the movement of wholesale prices. After 1963 the wholesale price indexes of the remaining EEC members also showed marked increases.

It has been asserted that the wholesale price index really is not an adequate measure of the general domestic price level, at least when used for international comparisons.[21] This assertion is based on the fact that wholesale price indexes generally are heavily weighted with internationally traded commodities, adjust fairly rapidly to international differentials, and usually move in a roughly parallel fashion. Hence a better measure of general price levels for use in determining international competitiveness, on the basis of price, might be the cost of living index, the wage index, or the GNP deflator.

However, it is evident that the consumer price indexes, hourly earnings indexes, and GNP price indexes of the EEC nations do not materially change the picture. Hourly earnings in manufacturing and consumer prices rose at a considerably more rapid rate in France than in the remaining EEC countries. This is especially true of consumer prices, which seem to follow the general pattern of wholesale prices. Similar statements may be made about the GNP implicit price deflator, presented in the Appendix, Table 6. All of the national price series seem to move in a roughly parallel manner with the exception of the French. Hence only in the case of France could the increase in the price level, relative to other EEC countries, have dampened exports and stimulated imports in intra-EEC trade. This may partly account for the extraordinarily high actual import figure for France in Table 17 and Appendix Table 12.

As mentioned earlier, it is also doubtful that the price effects due to currency revaluations had much impact on the total volume of intra-EEC trade during 1958-65. France devalued by 20 per cent in 1958, and Germany and the Netherlands revalued upward by 5 per cent in 1961. The French devaluation presumably dampened imports and stimulated exports in trade with other EEC countries, while the German and Dutch upward revaluations had the opposite effect. The total impact on over-all EEC trade probably was not very great, since the effects are mutually offsetting. In any case, they could be determined only if the price elasticities of import demand and export supply were known.

ECONOMIC DISTANCE

Another set of factors which could have affected intra-EEC trade relates to economic distance and, like changes in relative price levels and currency values, can be included in the residual of the intra-EEC trade function presented above. No matter how great the reduction of intra-EEC trade barriers or how rapid the rate of economic growth of the member countries, little increased trade could have resulted if the economic distance between them were prohibitive. Moreover, reduction of this economic distance between the EEC countries, if it were not associated with the formation of the Common Market, could have led to an expansion of intra-area trade quite apart from that induced by the EEC or other factors enumerated earlier.

Perhaps the only feasible way of estimating economic distance between countries consists of using the commodity trade statistics published by the OECD. The difference between 1) the f.o.b. average value of certain specific exports destined for specific countries, and 2) the c.i.f. value of these same goods as imports of the destination country has been taken as an appropriate indicator of economic distance.[22] This method can hardly be considered exact, primarily because time lags are bound to occur between the f.o.b. export and c.i.f. import valuations of commodities entering international trade which may affect the difference. But it is the best available approximation of economic distance between trading countries.

Beckerman has applied this method to the European scene and has ranked the principal trading partners of each European country in terms of economic distance as of 1956. It should be emphasized that these relationships may shift over time, especially with regard to Italy, as improvements are made in the European transport system which result in a lowering of transportation costs and, hence, in a shortening of economic distance. If the principal European trading partners of each EEC nation are ranked in terms of economic distance (shortest to longest), the following table results:

Table 18

Rankings of Countries in Order of Estimated Economic Distance from Selected Countries, 1956[23]

Belgium-Luxembourg	France	Germany	Italy	Netherlands
1. Netherlands	1. Belgium-Luxembourg	1. Austria	1. Switzerland	1. Belgium-Luxembourg
2. France	2. Germany	2. Switzerland	2. Austria	2. Germany
3. Germany	3. Netherlands	3. France	3. France	3. France
4. U.K.	4. U.K.	4. Netherlands	4. Germany	4. U.K.
5. Norway	5. Portugal	5. Belgium-Luxembourg	5. Greece	5. Norway
6. Denmark	6. Norway	6. Italy	6. Turkey	6. Sweden
7. Sweden	7. Sweden	7. Denmark	7. Portugal	7. Denmark
8. Portugal	8. Denmark	8. Sweden	8. U.K.	8. Portugal
9. Italy	9. Italy	9. U.K.	9. Netherlands	9. Italy
10. Greece	10. Greece	10. Norway	10. Belgium-Luxembourg	10. Greece
11. Turkey	11. Turkey	11. Portugal	11. Norway	11. Turkey
		12. Greece	12. Sweden	
		13. Turkey	13. Denmark	

It is clear that competition and hence trade will be carried through to a greater extent if the national markets are economically less separated. Great economic distance is just as effective in preventing a wide range of export goods from competing in a given market as high tariffs. The following table shows that, in the case of most EEC countries, the cumulated rankings of the remaining four Common Market nations or areas is substantially less than the cumulated rankings of the next four closest non-EEC European countries.

Table 19

Economic Distance Rankings Cumulated for Four EEC Countries and Nearest Four Non-EEC European Countries [24]

Country or Area	Cumulated Distance Rankings of EEC Countries	Cumulated Distance Rankings of the Four Nearest Non-EEC European Countries
Belgium-Luxembourg	15	22
France	15	22
Germany	18	18
Italy	26	14
Netherlands	15	22
Total EEC	89	98

In the case of the Low Countries and France, the economic distance to EEC partner countries is considerably less than the economic distance to the closest four non-EEC countries. Each of these nations is centrally located geographically and possesses efficient water and rail transport connections to the remaining three EEC countries in the region. Only the great economic distance with respect to Italy serves to raise the cumulated rankings of the EEC countries. For all three countries, the U.K. is the economically nearest non-EEC country. In the case of Germany the distance advantage of the EEC is by no means as clear. Austria and Switzerland are economically nearer than any EEC country, according to these calculations, although all Common Market countries are included in the next four positions. Italy has the least advantage, from the distance standpoint, with respect to the EEC. Austria, Switzerland, Greece, and Turkey all are fairly close to Italy; and the Alps pose a considerable economic distance handicap with respect to the remainder of the Common Market.

On the whole, however, it is clear, at least from the data presented here, that the Common Market is a fairly cohesive grouping of nations regarding economic distance. This implies that the reduction of trade barriers within the EEC and its ancillary effects probably had more of an expansionary influence on intra-EEC trade than if economic distances between the member countries had been greater. Based partly on economic distance, the U.N. Economic Commission for Europe has shown that the dependence of the EEC nations on intra-bloc exports has increased gradually from 1952 to 1959, and more rapidly thereafter.[25] Hence this factor may have been responsible for part of the increased regionalization of EEC trade shown earlier, although there is little reason for suspecting that it played a greater role after 1958 than before. It is not at all unreasonable to contend that the EEC common transport program, as well as cooperative EEC investments in transport facilities, were themselves partly responsible for any reduction of intra-community economic distance which can be shown to have occurred. Nevertheless, the magnitude of any such contribution is, and will remain, in doubt. Hence this consideration seems to detract only in a minor way from the conclusions drawn with regard to the Common Market's impact on internal trade.

INTRA-EEC TRADE IN PERSPECTIVE

So far, this chapter has been concerned primarily with trade developments taking place <u>within</u> the Common Market, and the case for the apparently substantial effect of the EEC has been built upon this foundation. The question thus comes to mind how intra-EEC trade growth during the 1958-63 period compared with world trade developments and especially how it compared with trade among other industrialized countries and among members of the European Free Trade Association.[26]

Table 20

Comparative Rates of Trade Growth, 1953-63 [27]
(in per cent per annum)

Years	Intra-EEC	Intra-EFTA	Intra-OECD* (exclud. EEC)	Developed*** Countries (exclud. EEC)	Intra-European OECD (exclud. EEC)	Intra-North America	World
1) 1953-1958	11.1	4.3	13.8	5.9	6.2	3.1	5.9
2) 1958-1963	18.3	8.8	5.8	7.8	8.2	3.9	7.7
3) Per cent increase**	64.9	104.7	-58.0	32.3	32.3	25.8	30.5

* Non-EEC OECD comprises Canada, United States, Austria, Denmark, Greece, Ireland, Norway, Portugal, Sweden, United Kingdom, and Yugoslavia.

** Row 2 less row 1 as a per cent of row 1.

*** Comprises non-EEC Western Europe, Canada, United States, Australia, New Zealand, South Africa, and Japan.

Table 21

Comparative Import and Export Shares and Intra-Trade Relative to Trade Among Developed* Countries: EEC and EFTA, 1953-63 [28]

Year	EEC Trade with EEC as a Per Cent of EEC Total Trade		EFTA Trade with EFTA as a Per Cent of EFTA Total Trade		Intra-EEC Trade as a Per Cent of Trade Among Developed Countries	Intra-EFTA Trade as a Per Cent of Trade Among Developed Countries
	Exports	Imports	Exports	Imports		
1953	28.4	26.3	19.0	17.2	11.9	6.8
1958	30.5	29.6	17.8	16.5	14.6	6.0
1963	42.4	38.9	19.8	15.1	21.4	5.8
Change, 1953-1958	7.4	12.5	-6.3	-4.1	22.7	-11.8
Change, 1958-1963	39.0	31.4	11.2	-8.5	46.6	-3.3

* North America, Western Europe, Australia, New Zealand, and Japan.

World trade generally grew more rapidly during the 1958-63 period than during 1953-58. Most probably, this occurred partly in response to a somewhat higher rate of economic growth in many of the world's trading nations during the second period. Moreover, there was a general movement toward convertibility on the part of many of these countries, and trade restrictions, in general, grew increasingly liberal. Of additional importance, the dollar-shortage era had come to an end and with it implicit and explicit discrimination against exports of the dollar area gradually diminished in importance.

Since the EEC stands out as the one extensive integration attempt, we would expect intra-EEC trade to grow more rapidly during the 1958-63 period, <u>ceteris paribus,</u> than world trade or trade among other industrialized countries, for the reason cited in earlier parts of this and preceding chapters. Similarly, according to the theoretical analysis of the two integration projects--EEC and EFTA-- intra-EEC trade growth would be considerably more rapid than intra-EFTA trade expansion during the period of time under consideration here.

The data on comparative trade growth is presented in the Appendix, Table 10, and summarized in Table 20.

It is clear that the rate of intra-EEC trade growth during 1958-63 was by far the highest of all groups of countries considered in this table. During the pre-EEC period, it was exceeded only by the rate of growth of trade among other OECD countries, which is primarily accounted for by the rapid expansion of trade between North America and the rest of Western Europe. Perhaps of greatest interest in Table 20 is the surprising jump in the rate of intra-EFTA trade growth after 1958, although this may in part be accounted for by the extremely low figure (when compared with intra-OECD or intra-EEC trade growth) for EFTA during 1953-58.

While on the surface it would seem that EFTA did have considerable impact on the volume of trade between the member countries, this notion is refuted by an analysis of import and export shares, presented in Table 21. Rather, it seems that the increase in the rate of intra-EFTA trade growth was part of a more general increase in the over-all rate of EFTA trade growth.

While the share of intra-trade rose considerably from 1958 to 1963 in the case of the EEC (by 39.0 per cent for exports and 31.4 per cent for imports), it rose only moderately for EFTA exports (11.2 per cent) and actually declined by 8.5 per cent for EFTA imports. On the whole, then, while intra-area trade clearly gained in significance relative to total trade in the EEC after 1958, no such tendency is evident in the case of EFTA. Similarly, intra-EEC trade gained substantially relative to total trade among developed countries, while intra-EFTA trade fell relatively during both 1953-58 and 1958-63.

Part of the difference in import and export shares between EEC and EFTA may be ascribed to the continuation of the Commonwealth Preference System by the U.K. and to the absence of a unified external tariff and trade policy in EFTA (i.e., the difference between a "free trade area" and a "customs union"); both factors would tend to support external trade growth as against internal trade growth. In part, this may explain the lack of initial effectiveness of the EFTA relative to the EEC, which has been so often asserted.

On the whole, the comparison of intra-EEC trade data with world trade developments seems to support the earlier analyses, and the conclusion that the formation of the EEC must have had substantial impact on Common Market trade patterns and growth remains essentially intact.

SUMMARY

In general, the empirical findings of this chapter support the <u>a priori</u> statements on the expected change in EEC trade patterns and growth, based on the theory of economic integration as applied to the European case, presented in earlier chapters. A number of different approaches have been taken in order to limit the weaknesses--and there are many--which might be inherent in any single method of analysis. Taken singly, each of the analyses imparts the feeling that the formation of the Common Market must have had a great deal to do with raising the rate of growth of intra-EEC trade and in shifting the direction of trade toward increasing inward-orientation. They seem to be indicative of the general direction and magnitude of change, even if the precise magnitude of the EEC effect cannot be determined.

Comparison of the average annual rates of growth of intra-EEC trade shows that, both in terms of current and constant prices, the rate of growth of internal Common Market trade was substantially higher during the post-EEC period than during the years immediately preceding it. This conclusion seems to hold, even after a number of more or less potent objections are applied, for both the EEC as a whole and for the member countries individually, and there is a good correspondence between the extent of intra-area trade expansion and the degree of tariff reduction.

Similarly, the several methods used to determine the extent of a shift in the direction of trade of the Common Market countries each supports the notion that there must have been a considerable EEC effect. This is equally true of the analysis of changes occurring in import and export shares during the post-EEC period, comparisons of changes in trade shares before and after 1958, the analysis of the rate of regionalization of imports and exports, as well as an analysis of changes in the weighted share indexes of total trade.

Eliminating the probable impact of changes of EEC real Gross National Product on intra-EEC trade by means of a partial average propensity to import, it was found that very little of the growth of intra-EEC trade, during the post-EEC period, can be explained by growth of real GNP in the member countries. Hence that part of intra-area trade growth remaining to be explained by factors associated with the EEC is very substantial. This conclusion was not materially affected by an analysis of the various price effects which occurred during the period under consideration, and was supported by an exposition of the role of economic distance in intra-EEC trade.

Finally, a comparison of intra-EEC and intra-EFTA trade developments showed that the changes which did occur were generally in line with the predictions of the theory of economic integration. The rate of growth of trade among EEC countries during the post-Common Market period was substantially higher than the rate of growth of intra-EFTA trade or of trade among a number of other groupings of trading nations. The same conclusion holds with regard to world trade in general, and to the importance of intra-trade relative to trade with all developed countries for both the EEC and EFTA, respectively.

While the results of the investigation pursued in this chapter largely support the a priori statements made earlier, it would certainly seem worthwhile to go somewhat more deeply into the question in order to determine the probable effect of economic integration on the volume and direction of intra-EEC trade for various different commodities and commodity groups. Such questions are dealt with in the following chapter.

Notes to Chapter 5

1. The export price index of each country is weighted by the percentage of intra-EEC trade held by that country for each year.

2. Data: Appendix Table 3. Deflator used: Appendix Table 4. Figures for 1958-65 are estimates.

3. A more technical point concerns the use of the years 1953, 1958, 1963, and 1965 in this study. There can be little question about the years 1953, 1963, and 1965; all were relatively "normal" with respect to cyclical swings in economic activity, while 1965 is used primarily because it is the latest year for which the data are available. The year 1958 presents a more difficult problem, since the rate of economic growth in most EEC countries slowed somewhat. Hence the rates of change in trade flows would tend to have a downward bias for the period 1953-58 and an upward bias for 1958-65. This is verified by an inspection of the tables in the Appendix. However, the slight recession does not seem to have had a very great impact on trade flows, so that the distortion of these figures does not seem to invalidate the conclusion drawn. Also, the fact that 1958 was the first year of the existence of the EEC (rather than the last year before its formation) does not seem to be of too much significance since none of the trade liberalization measures were implemented until the following year.

4. European Communities Statistical Office, Informations Statistiques, November-December, 1960, "Méthodes de Prévision du développement économique à long-terme" (Brussels: EEC).

5. Data: Current GNP, Appendix Table 5; Real GNP, Appendix Table 5 deflated by implicit GNP deflator given in Appendix Table 6, summarized in Appendix Table 7, in terms of U.S. dollars.

Alexander Lamfalussy, The United Kingdom and the Six (Homewood, Ill.: Richard D. Irwin, 1963).

6. See Alexander Lamfalussy, "Europe's Progress: Due to Common Market?" in L.B. Krause (ed.), The Common Market: Progress and Controversy (Englewood Cliffs, N.J.: Prentice-Hall, 1964), pp. 92-95.

7. Appendix Tables 2 and 3. Deflated by price indexes presented in Appendix Table 4.

8. Data: Table 10.

9. Data: Appendix Table 9. Figures for 1965 are estimates.

10. Change in percentage of exports (imports) going to EEC for years indicated.

11. See Erik Thorbecke, The Tendency Toward Regionalization in International Trade (The Hague: Martinus Nijhoff, 1960).

12. This analysis is carried out only for the two five-year periods immediately before and after the 1958 formation of the Common Market.

13. Data: Appendix Table 9.

14. Data: Appendix Table 9. An inspection of the trade 1965 estimates in Table 21 would suggest that these relationships tended in the same direction during 1958-65 as well as 1958-63.

15. This method was first developed by R.L. Major in National Institute Economic Review, August, 1962, pp. 24-36, and refined by P.J. Verdoorn and F.J.M. Meyer zu Schlochten, "Trade Diversion and Trade Creation in the Common Market," Intégration Européenne et Réalité Economique (Paris: OECD, 1964), pp. 95-138, and reprinted

in Central Planning Bureau Reprint Series, No. 93 (The Hague, 1965). See especially their Appendix, pp. 116-19. It is carried out only for the 1958-63 period due to the tentative nature of the 1965 data.

16. Ibid., p. 104.

17. Data: Appendix Tables 2 and 3 and OECD, Foreign Trade Statistics (Paris: OECD), various issues, 1953-65 inclusive. United Nations, Statistical Office, Statistical Papers, Series T, The Direction of International Trade (New York: U. N.), various issues, 1953-65 inclusive.

18. Data: GNP figures from Appendix Table 7, deflated by GNP implicit price deflators given in Appendix Table 6. Regional import figures from Appendix Table 3, deflated by regional import deflator given in Appendix Table 4. Projections for 1965 may be found in the Appendix, Table 11.

19. Data: Appendix Tables 6, 7, 8, and 10. Estimates for 1965 are presented in the Appendix, Table 12.

20. "Waehrung: Inflation via Bruessel," Der Spiegel (July 1, 1964), Vol. 18, No. 27, pp. 36-34.

21. See especially: Gottfried Haberler, A Survey of International Trade Theory (Princeton: International Finance Section, Department of Economics, Princeton University, 1961), pp. 48-50.

22. W. Beckerman, "Distance and the Pattern of Intra-European Trade," Review of Economics and Statistics, February, 1956.

23. Ibid., p. 35.

24. Rankings: See Table 17.

25. United Nations, Economic Commission for Europe, Economic Bulletin for Europe, Vol. 15, No. 1 (Geneva: U.N., August, 1963), p. 11.

26. These data relate only to the 1958-63 post-EEC period. Data for 1965 were unavailable at this writing and would have added little to the conclusions.

27. Data, in current prices, from Appendix Table 10. Data on "developed countries" from U. N., Statistical Yearbook, 1963, and Direction of International Trade, 1965.

28. Data: U. N., Statistical Yearbook, 1963, and Direction of International Trade, 1965.

CHAPTER 6 PATTERNS AND GROWTH OF INTRA-EEC TRADE: COMMODITIES

So far this study has dealt with growth and change in the direction of Common Market trade exclusively in aggregate terms. That is, an attempt was made to indicate the probable impact of the formation of the EEC, based on various analyses of the growth and direction of the value of total trade, in terms of current and, where possible, constant prices.

It should be clear, however, that the effect of the Common Market on trade flows must have varied substantially from commodity to commodity. This was already broadly indicated in Chapters 2, 3, and 4, and is based on a number of important considerations. First, the impact of intra-EEC tariff reductions affects the volume and direction of intra-area trade in a particular commodity, or group of commodities, according to the price elasticity of demand (or, more narrowly, the "tariff elasticity of demand"). Second, the degree of applicability of the EEC trade liberalization program to a given commodity group is critical. Whereas it may have stimulated the rate of growth and increased inward-orientation of total trade, this stimulus may have been limited primarily to certain commodities. Agricultural commodities have already been mentioned as notable exceptions to general intra-EEC trade liberalization.

Third, while tariff reductions on intra-area trade in certain commodities may have been implemented, other considerations may have successfully impeded an expansion of trade and a shift in favor of the most efficient suppliers. Labeling and packaging regulations, health and safety standards, collusion and cartel practices, as well as deliberate complication of customs formalities are examples in this category. Many of these impediments are obviously difficult, if not impossible, to bring to light since many are implemented in a clandestine manner. Others were eliminated in connection with various Common Market programs and could thus have had an impact on intra-EEC trade, quite apart from the general removal of internal tariffs.

Finally, a number of fiscal considerations have been identified earlier as barriers to trade. Hence the national indirect taxation systems, which were left substantially intact during the entire post-EEC period, could have effectively prevented trade in certain commodities. Similarly, national tax measures implemented either as part of fiscal policy or for the express purpose of suppressing imports, could have had some effect in certain areas.

At the same time, the various non-tariff factors cited earlier as having a probable positive impact on intra-EEC trade doubtlessly differed in their effect on trade in various commodities. Expectations, integration of transport facilities, establishment of EEC-wide operations by firms, increased labor and capital mobility, and other such forces fall into this category.

All of these considerations seem to justify a more detailed analysis of EEC trade patterns and growth and a disaggregation of over-all trade, first, by broad commodity groups and, second, in the form of selected individual commodities. Moreover, this analysis should serve to confirm the conclusions reached earlier and based on the analysis of total trade.

BROAD COMMODITY GROUPS

Perhaps the best way to disaggregate total EEC trade by commodity groups is to make use of the Standard International Trade Classification (SITC) data, published by the United Nations. Although the data are at times difficult to handle, they are continuous and comparable over time. The broadest possible classification scheme uses single-digit totals and, combining those commodity groups likely to be affected in a similar way by the Common Market, the following commodity classes are derived:[1]

SITC 0 + 1 .....food, beverages, and tobacco
2 .....crude materials, inedible, except fuels
3 .....mineral fuels, lubricants, and related materials

4 ..... animal and vegetable oils and fats
5 ..... chemicals
7 ..... machinery and transport equipment
6 + 8 ..... other manufactured goods

We would expect some commodities in SITC classes 0 and 1 (food, beverages, and tobacco) to come under the EEC agriculture regulations, and hence not to be fully subject to the impact of reduced internal tariffs and quotas. Nevertheless, trade in beverages, tobacco, and many highly processed food items was largely liberalized and not hindered by the slow progress achieved in the agricultural area. Moreover, we would expect little impact of the EEC on trade in SITC group 4 (animal and vegetable oils and fats) due to the special agricultural regulations.

Mineral fuels, lubricants, and related materials (SITC 3) are largely supplied, in crude form, externally to the EEC. Once within the Common Market, however, these commodities are fully subject to the regulations governing internal trade. The one notable exception is coal, which comes under the European Coal and Steel Community trade regulations. The effects of integration in this area should, however, have been well under way by the time the EEC was formed in 1958. Since all EEC countries possess oil refineries, there is little reason to expect high internal trade growth in crude oil (except for transit shipments through such facilities as the Bordeaux-Cologne pipeline), although considerable trade expansion might be expected in the refined product. The same holds true of the products of natural gas deposits which have been exploited in Italy, the Netherlands, and elsewhere in the EEC over the past decade.

Most of the trade growth in response to the Common Market would have occurred in three categories: chemicals, transport equipment and machinery, and other manufactures (SITC 5, 7, and 6+8). This is true primarily for three reasons. First, many of these commodities would seem to have a high price elasticity of demand. This would be especially true of chemicals and certain manufactures and least true of goods which are highly differentiated in terms of quality, especially in technology. Second, most of these goods are of relatively high total value-added, and a given increase in the physical volume of trade would cause a substantial increase in the money value of trade. If an increasing proportion of intra-EEC trade were carried on in these particular commodity groups, this would be another source of expansion. Finally, virtually all of the individual goods continued in these classes were fully subject to the EEC internal trade liberalization program.

The same general a priori statements made above in the case of fuels and lubricants also hold true, although to a lesser degree, for non-fuel crude materials (SITC 2) and substantial trade growth might be expected in this area, not only in direct response to increasingly free trade within the EEC but also as a secondary effect of increased trade in chemicals and manufactures as well as, of course, GNP growth.

In order to determine the degree to which trade growth of each of the commodity groups influenced the over-all growth and composition of intra-EEC trade, three questions must be answered: 1) How much of the total 1958-63 real intra-EEC trade growth was attributable to the expansion of trade in each of the commodity groups? 2) To what extent did the commodity composition of intra-EEC trade change during the 1958-63 period? 3) How did the rates of growth of the various commodity groups compare with one another and with the rate of growth of over-all trade? Once this has been done, the answers to each of these questions may be compared with the corresponding performance of commodity trade growth during the pre-EEC 1953-58 period and significant changes may be noted.[2]

COMPARATIVE COMMODITY TRADE GROWTH

From 1958 to 1963, the value of annual intra-EEC trade grew by $914.9 million (see Table 22). Of this total trade growth, manufactures and chemicals accounted for 73.3 per cent, agricultural commodities and their derivatives 10.5 per cent, and raw materials and fuels 8.9 per cent. A total of 7.3 per cent is attributable to trade growth in goods not classified under any of these categories and to statistical discrepancies in the data. Hence those commodities which were fully subject to the intra-EEC trade liberalization program accounted for well over three fourths of the growth of intra-area trade. As we shall see below, however, this supplies us with very little evidence as to the effectiveness of the

Common Market.

At the same time, the commodity composition of intra-EEC trade changed to some degree, as Table 22 shows.

Table 22

Commodity Composition of Intra-EEC Trade, 1958 and 1963 [3]

Commodity Group (SITC Code)*	Intra-EEC Trade 1958	Per Cent of Total	Intra-EEC Trade 1963	Per Cent of Total
0 + 1	908.5	13.4	1,823.4	11.6
2	495.4	7.3	1,121.2	7.1
3	743.9	11.0	911.0	5.8
4	33.5	0.5	63.9	0.4
5	485.6	7.2	1,105.2	7.0
7	1,513.9	22.3	4,299.0	27.4
6 + 8	2,456.7	36.2	5,598.5	35.6
Misc.**	149.7	2.1	797.8	5.1
Total	6,787.2	100.0	15,720.0	100.0

* SITC Code:
- 0 + 1 ... food, beverages, and tobacco
- 2 ... crude materials, inedible, except fuels
- 3 ... mineral fuels, lubricants, and related materials
- 4 ... animal and vegetable oils and fats
- 5 ... chemicals
- 7 ... machinery and transport equipment
- 6 + 8 ... other manufactured goods

** Miscellaneous: All goods not included in SITC Code 0 to 8 and statistical discrepancy.

The relative importance of trade in machinery and transport equipment grew considerably during the period after the formation of the Common Market, while that of agricultural commodities, mineral fuels, and related materials declined. The relative shares of the other commodities changed but little. While the absolute value of trade in all of these areas grew substantially, their relative importance declined or remained stable due to the rapid growth of trade in machinery and transport equipment. Unless other considerations such as changes in supply conditions played a prominent role, this would seem to suggest that the Common Market had its greatest impact in this particular area.

Alternatively, an analysis of average annual rates of trade growth for the various commodity groups also shows that trade in machinery and transport equipment grew most rapidly by far and that it is the only commodity group which exceeded the rate of growth of over-all trade (Table 23).

Table 23

Average Annual Rates of Intra-EEC Trade Growth by Commodity Groups, 1958-63[4]
(per cent per year, current prices)

Average Annual Rate of Trade Growth	SITC CODE							Total
	0+1	2	3	4	5	7	6+8	Trade
	15.0	17.8	4.1	13.8	17.8	23.2	17.9	18.3

Trade in agricultural commodities grew least rapidly (food, beverages, tobacco, and animal and vegetable oils and fats) with the exception of mineral fuels and related materials. As noted earlier, however, the latter category is subject to special conditions and would not be subject to rapid growth under any conditions.

Based on the above information, it is clear that trade in trucks, buses, automobiles, and industrial machinery was responsible for the greatest portion of the growth of intra-EEC trade during the time period under study here. In addition, the commodity composition of trade between the Common Market countries moved in favor of this particular commodity group. However, we would have little basis for asserting that the Common Market affected trade in this group of goods most profoundly if other factors can be shown to be responsible for a substantial part of this development. For example, does GNP growth favor imports in machinery and transport equipment more than other goods categories? Or, is there any evidence to the effect that trade among countries of roughly equal industrial development will grow most rapidly in those goods which they all produce and consume?[5] The impact of factors such as these can be brought out by means of an analysis similar to, but less comprehensive than, that used in the preceding chapter. If it can be shown that there are significant changes which occurred in the rates of growth of the various commodity groups or in the commodity composition of trade during 1958-63 with respect to 1953-58, we can at least indicate the existence of some sort of Common Market effect. This, of course, rests on the validity of the proposition, presented in Chapter 5, that the relevant variables (GNP growth, price level change, etc.) did not alter extensively in the rate or nature of movement.

CHANGE IN COMMODITY TRADE, 1953-58 AND 1958-63

We mentioned earlier that growth of trade in manufactures and chemicals contributed over three fourths of the growth of total trade during 1958-63. These three commodity groups combined (SITC Code 5, 7, and 6+8) also contributed about 77 per cent of total trade growth during the pre-EEC 1953-58 time period. The contribution of general manufactures and chemicals declined from one period to the next, while that of machinery and transport equipment rose to some degree. Similarly, the contribution of crude materials rose from 1953-58 to 1958-63, while that of all other commodity groups declined, most spectacularly in the case of mineral fuels, lubricants, and related materials. The relevant data are presented in Table 24 below.

These data would seem to support the indications, evident in all of the earlier analyses, that the EEC effect was most pronounced in the case of machinery and transport equipment. There is little reason to believe, at least on the surface, that this group of goods should have contributed more to intra-community trade growth during the years after the EEC was formed than before, in the absence of the Common Market.

Table 24

Contributions of Major Commodity Groups to Intra-EEC Trade Growth, 1953-58 and 1958-63 (millions of U.S. dollars and per cent) [6]

Commodity Groups (SITC Code)*	Trade Growth 1953-58	Per Cent of Total	Trade Growth 1958-63	Per Cent of Total
0 + 1	339.2	11.9	914.9	10.2
2	161.7	5.7	625.8	7.0
3	185.8	6.5	167.1	1.9
4	12.8	0.4	30.4	0.3
5	242.1	8.5	609.6	6.8
7	805.9	28.3	2,785.1	31.2
6 + 8	1,135.5	39.8	3,141.8	35.3
Misc.**	-32.5	-1.1	648.1	7.3
Total	2,850.5	100.0	8,932.8	100.0

* SITC Code: 0 + 1 ... food, beverages, and tobacco
2 ... crude materials, inedible, except fuels
3 ... mineral fuels, lubricants, and related materials
4 ... animal and vegetable oils and fats
5 ... chemicals
7 ... machinery and transport equipment
6 + 8 ... other manufactured goods

** Miscellaneous: All goods not included in SITC Code 0 to 8 and statistical discrepancy.

This idea is further supported by the analysis and comparison of the rates of intra-area trade growth for the various commodity groups during the two successive periods 1953-58 and 1958-63. Table 25 shows that the rate of growth of intra-EEC trade in machinery and transport equipment was considerably higher during the second, post-EEC period than during the earlier period. In fact, the increase in the average annual rate of growth from one period to the next was greater in the case of this commodity group than for any other, with the exception of trade in raw materials excluding fuels. The latter shows the most substantial increase in the rate of growth, although in absolute terms it was still well below the growth of trade in machinery and transport equipment during the 1958-63 period.

Table 25

Comparative Rates of Intra-EEC Trade Growth
by Commodities, 1953-58 and 1958-63
(in per cent per year) [7]

Commodity Group (SITC Code)*	1953-58	1958-63	Difference
0 + 1	9.8	15.0	+5.2
2	8.2	17.8	+9.6
3	5.9	4.1	-1.8
4	10.1	13.8	+3.7
5	14.8	17.8	+3.0
7	16.4	23.2	+6.8
6 + 8	13.2	17.9	+4.7
Over-all	11.5	18.3	+6.8

* Commodity SITC Code: See note to Table 24.

From the above analyses, then, we might be led to conclude that the growth of total intra-EEC trade during the post-EEC period was primarily due to the expansion of trade in those commodity groups most affected by the trade provisions of the Common Market. Moreover, it is clear that the increase in the rate of over-all trade growth from 1953-58 to 1958-63 is primarily attributable to more rapid growth of the intra-area trade of these same commodities. It was also found that the commodity composition of intra-community trade changed from 1958 to 1963 substantially in favor of that commodity group which appears to have been most profoundly affected by the Common Market: machinery and transport equipment. This appears to be true in spite of the fact that there was already a tendency for trade among the Common Market countries to be increasingly concentrated in this group of goods. While the importance of machinery and transport equipment increased during 1953-58 as well, so did that of other manufactures and chemicals. In contrast, the latter actually declined in importance from 1958 to 1963, and of all commodity groups, only machinery and transport equipment appears to have assumed an increasingly important role.

Table 26

Commodity Composition of Intra-EEC Trade, 1953, 1958, and 1963 [8] (in per cent)

Commodity Group (SITC Code)*	1953	1958	Change 1953-58	1963	Change 1958-63
0 + 1	14.5	13.4	-0.9	11.6	-1.8
2	8.5	7.3	-1.2	7.1	-2.0
3	14.2	11.0	-3.2	5.8	-5.2
4	0.5	0.5	-0 -	0.4	-0.1
5	6.2	7.2	+1.0	7.0	-0.2
7	18.0	22.3	+4.3	27.4	+5.1
6 + 8	33.6	36.2	+2.6	35.6	-0.6
Misc.	4.5	2.1	-2.4	5.1	+3.0
Total	100.0	100.0		100.0	

* SITC Commodity Code: See note to Table 24.

There is yet another way to analyze the effects of the EEC on the value of intra-area trade in the various commodity groups. Chapter 3 pointed out that, as the Common Market trade liberalization program draws to completion, certain shifts will take place in the supply-demand relationships among the member countries. The previously high-tariff countries would have to undertake the most substantial tariff cuts and would presumably expand imports from the rest of the EEC to a considerable extent. The reasons given for this were, among others, the income effect and the substitution effect: The assumed declining prices cause consumers or users to have more effective disposable income, and at the same time they would shift their purchases from high-priced domestic goods to low-priced imported goods. On the supply side, those countries possessing the most efficient producers would begin to obtain a larger share of the total EEC market.

SUPPLY AND ABSORPTION

The question of reallocation of production will be explored in greater detail in the following chapter. However, this general notion is useful at this point by helping to determine the effects of the EEC on the value of trade in the various commodity groups. If a significant reallocation of production took place which is attributable to the EEC, then an increasing share of total intra-area exports should go to the most efficient suppliers while, at the same time, these countries should absorb, or import, a decreasing share of total intra-EEC trade. The reverse is true, of course, in the case of those countries possessing the least efficient suppliers. If the analysis presented earlier in this chapter is correct, then the supply-demand shifts which occurred during 1958-63 should have been most pronounced in the case of those commodity groups which, according to the data on trade and commodity composition, seem to have been most affected by the EEC.

As the data in Table 27 show, Germany was both the dominant supplier and the dominant importer with respect to total intra-EEC trade in 1953, 1958, and 1963. Italy gained gradually as a supplier, during the earlier period, and more rapidly during the post-EEC period. At the same time, its share of total imports declined during 1953-58 but rose considerably during 1958-63. The Netherlands' share declined slightly over the entire period on both the import and the export side, which was also true, to a greater degree, in the case of Belgium-Luxembourg. French exports declined as a per cent of total trade during 1953-58 but rose during 1958-63, while imports rose slightly in importance over the entire period. Thus the proportion of total intra-EEC trade supplied, during 1953-58, by Italy, Germany, and the Netherlands grew at the expense of France and Belgium-Luxembourg; in contrast,

Table 27

Percentage of Total Intra-EEC Commodity Trade Supplied and Absorbed by the Member Countries, 1953, 1958, and 1963[9]

SITC Class	Year	Belgium-Lux. Suppl.	Belgium-Lux. Abs.	France Suppl.	France Abs.	Germany Suppl.	Germany Abs.	Italy Suppl.	Italy Abs.	Netherlands Suppl.	Netherlands Abs.
	1953	7.6	24.5	12.3	10.0	3.8	53.9	23.6	5.4	52.6	5.1
0+1	1958	9.7	17.1	13.7	10.1	7.8	55.5	23.5	8.6	55.3	8.8
	1963	13.1	13.1	20.7	12.6	6.3	52.9	18.6	13.2	51.2	8.2
	1953	23.0	4.3	40.2	13.9	13.0	37.8	6.9	23.0	16.8	20.9
2	1958	18.1	13.1	36.5	15.5	18.8	34.4	7.3	21.2	19.4	15.8
	1963	19.8	23.3	35.3	10.9	18.4	30.2	6.3	12.5	20.2	23.1
	1953	17.0	17.7	16.5	36.4	55.9	14.4	0.6	17.1	10.1	14.5
3	1958	14.4	26.1	8.1	37.8	55.4	16.1	2.3	5.7	19.9	14.3
	1963	14.0	24.8	3.2	31.0	47.9	21.2	6.1	5.5	28.8	17.3
	1953	19.5	12.1	9.2	2.4	8.0	49.3	1.0	27.5	62.3	8.7
4	1958	16.4	21.5	10.1	6.9	19.7	37.9	2.7	18.5	51.1	15.2
	1963	15.2	17.5	13.4	26.9	24.4	27.7	4.1	14.1	42.8	13.8

Table 27, Continued

SITC Class	Year	Belgium-Lux. Suppl.	Belgium-Lux. Abs.	France Suppl.	France Abs.	Germany Suppl.	Germany Abs.	Italy Suppl.	Italy Abs.	Netherlands Suppl.	Netherlands Abs.
	1953	17.4	30.2	23.1	14.7	41.4	14.5	4.6	15.1	13.5	25.5
5	1958	14.9	27.1	20.1	16.3	42.9	15.8	6.0	16.9	16.1	23.9
	1963	12.7	20.1	19.6	21.5	42.1	19.2	8.7	19.9	15.9	19.3
	1953	10.6	28.7	11.9	20.4	61.0	5.7	5.8	16.7	10.7	28.5
7	1958	13.6	25.3	11.6	20.1	53.4	13.8	9.9	10.7	11.5	30.0
	1963	13.0	19.8	12.2	19.1	51.4	14.8	12.2	20.6	11.2	25.7
	1953	35.1	20.8	20.6	9.2	24.8	25.1	5.6	11.9	13.9	33.0
6+8	1958	32.4	17.3	14.3	15.8	24.0	31.6	8.9	8.4	15.4	26.8
	1963	27.7	15.3	17.0	18.2	30.6	30.3	12.0	14.2	12.6	21.9
	1953	21.7	23.7	18.6	16.0	32.9	24.3	7.7	13.5	19.1	22.4
Total	1958	20.0	21.5	16.6	18.1	35.1	27.9	8.9	10.1	19.5	22.4
	1963	18.6	17.1	19.1	19.8	34.3	27.6	11.3	15.8	16.7	19.6

during the post-EEC period the proportion supplied by France and Italy grew at the expense of exports of the remaining member countries; only in the case of Italy did it grow during both periods. The proportion of total intra-area trade absorbed by the Benelux countries declined during both periods while that of France increased during both 1953-58 and 1958-63. Germany's share of total imports rose during the earlier period and then declined while the reverse was true in the case of Italy.

It is true, then, that the percentage of total trade absorbed by the high-tariff countries (France and Italy) rose while that of the low-tariff countries declined after the EEC was formed, which meets the predictions of the theoretical analysis.

In the case of food, beverages, and tobacco, the Netherlands was the Common Market's dominant supplier, although it was Belgium-Luxembourg and France which gained substantially after the formation of the EEC. The increases in these countries' exports were absorbed largely by Italy.

The dominant supplier of raw materials was France and, although no discernable pattern is evident on the export side, the Benelux countries increased their relative absorption to a very large degree.

Germany retained its position as dominant supplier of mineral fuels and lubricants, but it as well as Belgium-Luxembourg and France lost considerably to Italy and the Netherlands. Just as in the case of agricultural exports, the Benelux countries remained the dominant suppliers of animal and vegetable oils and fats, but lost a great deal of ground to the rest of the Common Market after 1958. Chemicals seem to be a special case with Germany, the dominant supplier, strengthening its position both before and after the Common Market was formed at the expense of the other EEC countries with the exception of Italy, which gained substantially. The German-Italian increase in chemicals exports seems to have been absorbed primarily by France.

In the case of machinery and transport equipment, Germany again was the dominant supplier, but lost steadily to the rest of the Common Market, especially Italy. It is perhaps significant that Belgium-Luxembourg was the Common

Market's dominant supplier of other manufactures during both 1953 and 1958 but lost its position to Germany in 1963. The declining share of Belgium-Luxembourg exports was taken over by Germany and Italy and, in turn, was in large measure absorbed by France.

It is evident that the dominant supplier country in every case (with the exception of chemicals) declined in its share of intra-EEC exports both before and after the advent of the Common Market, though generally less significantly after 1958. Equally significant is the fact that the shares of the dominant importers also declined in each instance after the formation of the Common Market. Both of these observations indicate a much more even distribution of trade among the Common Market countries, on both the import and the export side, after the formation of the EEC. The first opposes the theory that the pre-EEC dominant supplier will substantially increase his share of exports to the Common Market as tariff barriers to his exports are reduced.[10] It is apparent that changes in supply conditions brought about a more even distribution of the member countries' intra-EEC export shares before 1958 and that this substantially reduced the share of the dominant supplier. With internal trade liberalization after 1958, the rate of deterioration of the dominant supplier's position generally slowed as it became more competitive in the domestic markets of the remaining member countries. Thus, Table 27 does seem to show an EEC effect, but one which operates in a way quite different from what was expected on an *a priori* basis.

The deterioration in the absorption shares of the dominant importers takes a more predictable course. One would have expected the lowest-tariff countries to be the dominant importers, and for them to lose this position gradually as the intra-area tariffs of the other members were reduced. The data show that this actually occurred after 1958, and that before the formation of the EEC there was a tendency for the dominant importers to strengthen their relative absorption of certain commodity groups (agricultural products, fuels and lubricants, and machinery and transport equipment). Finally, it is clear that the most pronounced deterioration in the relative absorption of those commodity groups cited above as being most likely to be affected by the Common Market occurred in the case of the low-tariff countries (Benelux and Germany), while the greatest increase in the absorption share generally occurred in the case of the high-tariff countries (Italy and France). The relative supply and absorption based on total intra-EEC trade shows that, while Germany remained the dominant exporter and importer, its position in both categories declined after the formation of the Common Market.

Thus far, this chapter has largely supported both the theoretical arguments and the analysis of total trade presented in the previous chapter. It was shown that those commodity groups broadly subjected to the EEC tariff reduction program underwent rapid growth during 1958-63 and that this growth exceeded that of the pre-EEC period. Moreover, it was these same goods which attracted an increasing share of the over-all commodity composition of intra-EEC trade during 1958-63. It was also shown that the supply and absorption shares behaved roughly in accordance with the theoretical indications, but that the idea of increasing supplier dominance is not borne out by the facts. However, a great deal more could be learned if a finer commodity breakdown were possible, so that the behavior of trade in individual commodities could be studied.

TRADE IN SELECTED COMMODITIES

Clearly, it would be useful to have an analysis such as that presented above for each individual commodity. One could then determine precisely where the EEC effect had its greatest impact and what other factors besides tariff reductions may have played a role. But such an analysis is clearly beyond the scope of this study and it is indicated here merely as a possible fruitful object of future research.

It should be sufficient, in order to extend and confirm the results of the earlier analyses, to take a relatively small sample of commodities for analysis. Most of these goods should have been included under the EEC tariff-reduction program, although two or three commodities not affected might be used as a control group. It would be useful if most of the commodities selected assumed a relatively important role in intra-EEC trade in general, and particularly in those broad commodity groups which were designated earlier as having played a major part in the growth of trade and, in the change in trade patterns, which occurred between the Common Market countries during the 1958-63 period. Obviously, no attempt at randomness in the selection of sample commodities will be made.

The goods selected are as follows, with the corresponding three-digit identification of the Standard International Trade Classification system:[11]

Wheat flours and meal	(046)
Manufactured tobacco	(122)
Alcoholic beverages	(112)
Synthetic and regenerated fibers	(266)
Organic chemicals	(512)
Glassware	(665)
Metalworking machinery	(715)
Electric power machinery, switch-gear, etc.	(721)
Pharmaceutical products	(541)
Road motor vehicles	(732)
Footwear	(851)
Furniture	(821)

Unlike trade by commodity groups, it is possible to obtain quantity data for each of the goods listed, so that the problem of price changes is no longer of concern. All data are given in metric tons and, although it is conceivable there might be changes in the weight of individual commodities--so that weight would cease to be a reliable indicator of unit-volume--it is nevertheless somewhat unlikely that they would be substantial or that they would affect the results of the analysis to any marked degree.

Table 16 in the Appendix presents the relevant data for the trade of the six EEC nations in these commodities, both with each other and with the rest of the world, for the years 1954, 1958, and 1963. The year 1954 is chosen here, instead of 1953 as in all previous analyses, because pre-1954 trade of the EEC countries in certain commodities, particularly tobacco, was virtually nil and hence would make it impossible to carry out comparative studies in the growth and direction of trade.

Since little liberalization of trade in wheat flours and meal occurred from 1958 to 1963, we would expect no systematic reaction to the Common Market. Rather, trade in this commodity was subject to bilateral negotiations until

1958 and thereafter became subject to the EEC agricultural regulations, which had shown little progress by 1963.[12] This meant simply that deficiencies in domestic production were met by imports from other countries at the discretion of the national authorities, and that this was equally true in 1954, 1958, and 1963. The administratively controlled nature of trade in wheat flours and meal is demonstrated in Table 28 and, while intra-area trade in 1958 was enormous when compared with 1954, it was much less in 1963. Although not carried out here, an analysis of trade in this commodity during the intervening years would show equally great fluctuations, not based on anything except the administrative control of imports.

A similar problem, although less severe, is encountered in the case of trade in tobacco. France and Italy had state monopolies, established primarily for the purpose of raising public revenues, which possessed exclusive rights to the sale and distribution of tobacco products in their respective countries. Hence they were naturally reluctant to allow the liberal importation of tobacco products--a policy which was not modified by agreement within the EEC until 1963. Despite the substantial reduction of internal barriers to trade, therefore, the rate of growth of trade in this commodity did not increase with respect to the rate which prevailed during 1954-58, although the latter was itself very high.

Those commodities fully subject to the EEC trade liberalization program all underwent rapid expansion in intra-EEC trade after the Common Market was formed in 1958. In each case as well, this trade growth was considerably in excess of the average annual rate of trade growth during the pre-EEC period. Consumer goods categories such as furniture, footwear, glassware, alcoholic beverages, and automobiles all showed marked increases in the rate of trade growth from the first to the second period. This was also true of metalworking machinery, synthetic fibers, and organic chemicals among producer's goods. The increase in the rate of trade growth was least apparent in the case of electric power equipment and pharmaceutical products.

It is perhaps significant that those commodities which might be considered price-elastic (e.g., organic chemicals and glassware) rose greatly in the rate of trade growth, while those which could be price-inelastic (e.g., electric power

Table 28

Average Annual Rates of Intra-EEC Trade Growth in Selected Commodities and Tariff Reductions[13]

Commodity	Growth Rate 1954-58	Tariff Reduction* 1958-63 From	To	Percentage Points	Growth Rate 1958-63
Wheat flours and meal	161.0		None		(-60.5)
Manufactured tobacco	29.0	162.2	64.9	97.3	23.3
Alcoholic beverages	7.5	35.3	14.1	21.2	17.7
Synthetic fibers	18.9	15.0	6.0	9.0	28.6
Organic chemicals	7.7	17.3	6.9	10.4	23.2
Glassware	2.5	24.0	9.6	14.4	14.5
Metalworking machinery	4.4	9.9	4.0	5.9	22.6
Electric power equipment	10.1	13.3	5.3	8.0	11.4
Pharmaceutical products	21.4	14.7	5.9	8.8	23.5
Road motor vehicles	18.6	28.7	11.5	17.2	28.9
Footwear	16.8	20.0	8.0	12.0	29.3
Furniture	18.5	18.0	7.2	10.8	30.8

* Tariff reduction: Initial tariffs are the arithmetic averages of national duties in 1956. Where different tariff levels are included in the tariff for a given commodity, the resulting commodity tariff is the weighted mean of the individual sub-group tariffs, weights being the relative importance of each sub-group for EEC trade in that commodity.

Terminal tariffs are the initial tariffs, calculated as above, with an over-all 60% reduction applied. Hence terminal tariffs are 40% of initial tariff levels, as explained in Chapter 2.

Percentage-point decline constitutes initial tariff less terminal tariff.

equipment, pharmaceutical products) did not. If this were true, some statements could be made concerning the effects of tariff reductions on intra-EEC trade, especially if the respective elasticities were known.

Moreover, whereas GNP growth clearly must have affected trade in each of these commodities, the analysis presented in Chapter 5 showed that the rate of real GNP growth of the Common Market countries did not in fact increase markedly from 1954-58 to 1958-63. Hence it could have done little to bring about the increase in the rate of commodity trade growth presented here. In contrast, changing supply conditions could have had something to do with it, although it is doubtful that such changes were more pronounced during the latter period than during 1954-58.

The comparison of trade growth rates, and its implication of a substantial EEC effect over a broad range of commodities, is generally supported by the corresponding data relating to the direction of trade (Table 29). On the whole, imports of the EEC countries were far more inwardly oriented than exports in virtually all of the commodities under consideration during 1954, 1958, and 1963. Moreover, whereas the inward orientation of exports increased only slightly from 1954 to 1958, and substantially from 1958 to 1963, change in the direction of imports behaved quite differently. While the regionalization of imports was considerable during the pre-EEC period, it was hardly apparent from 1958 to 1963.

The most dramatic increases in the regionalization of exports during 1958-63 occurred in the case of furniture, footwear, road motor vehicles, metalworking machinery, alcoholic beverages, and manufactured tobacco. It declined substantially in the case of drugs. On the import side, it was only in tobacco, alcoholic beverages, synthetic fibers, and glassware that a significant increase occurred in regionalization, while it declined in the case of drugs and metalworking machinery. Hence the impact of the EEC on trade patterns was most apparent in the case of these goods; and, since export regionalization was, on the whole, considerably more pronounced than import regionalization, charges of EEC discrimination against outside producers seem to lose some of their validity. This is the same conclusion reached in Chapter 5 with respect to total trade.

Table 29

Intra-EEC Trade, as a Per Cent of Members' Total Trade in Selected Commodities[14]

Commodity	Exports*			Imports*		
	1954	1958	1963	1954	1958	1963
Wheat flours and meal	0.8	15.1	1.4	1.8	46.5	18.2
Manufactured tobacco	29.9	43.5	52.1	41.0	56.0	74.6
Alcoholic beverages	26.1	34.7	51.6	11.1	11.3	22.6
Synthetic fibers	7.9	11.4	20.4	32.5	44.7	58.7
Organic chemicals	32.9	36.2	36.4	45.3	37.5	37.9
Glassware	42.7	42.1	46.9	69.3	67.5	74.9
Metalworking machinery	26.2	20.8	38.6	40.8	59.0	57.9
Electric power equipment	21.0	22.8	22.8	66.0	68.8	69.3
Drugs	10.2	14.6	8.9	23.4	42.5	31.0
Road motor vehicles	22.1	19.6	38.5	56.9	75.2	77.9
Footwear	19.4	21.6	39.4	56.5	58.6	61.7
Furniture	26.3	35.4	62.2	77.0	66.9	70.4
Average of 12 goods	22.1	26.5	34.9	43.5	52.9	54.6

* All trade figures based on data in metric tons.

Based on the data presented in Table 29, an import and export share index analysis may be made of the pattern of EEC trade in these twelve commodities for the period 1954-63. Letting the percentage of intra-area trade in 1954 equal 100, we can calculate the corresponding index for 1958 and, by dividing the difference by the number of intervening years, get an idea of the movement toward or away from the inward orientation of trade. The same analysis may be made for 1963 with respect to the base year 1958, and the results for the periods 1954-58 and 1958-63, respectively, may then be compared in order to identify any significant difference which might be attributable to the Common Market. The results of these calculations are presented in Table 30 below.

On the export side (omitting the category 046--wheat flours and meal--for reasons cited earlier) it is evident that regionalization during 1958-63 was greatest in the case of furniture, footwear, road motor vehicles, metalworking machinery, and synthetic fibers (SITC: 821, 851, 732, 715, and 266, respectively). It should be noted that, in the case of each of these commodities, the increased inward orientation of exports apparent during 1958-63 was greater--often substantially greater--than that evidenced during the pre-EEC period. In addition, regionalization of exports was also greater during 1958-63 than during 1954-58 in the case of glassware and alcoholic beverages, but declined in the case of manufactured tobacco, organic chemicals, electric power machinery, and drugs. Exports of drugs, in fact, showed a marked decline in inward orientation during the post-EEC period.

Hence it seems that, of the commodities presented here, the impact of the EEC on the regionalization of exports was most apparent in the case of SITC classes 821, 851, 732, 715, and 266--furniture, footwear, road motor vehicles, metalworking machinery, and synthetic fibers.

In contrast, the inward orientation of imports grew to a far smaller degree in the case of most of the commodities selected for analysis. Only in the case of alcoholic beverages was the degree of regionalization far more pronounced during 1958-63 than during 1954-58. Most of the commodities which increased in the degree of inward orientation on the export side, from the former to the latter period, also showed similar movement on the import side. It is again interesting that, while the regionalization of imports of drugs was considerable during 1954-58, it was negative from 1958 to 1963: Since this occurred both for imports and exports, factors other than the Common Market must have been the determining ones in the case of this particular commodity.

From this analysis of changes in import and export patterns of the Common Market countries for selected goods, there develops some support for the idea, already established in the first half of this chapter, that the commodities most likely to be affected by the reduction of intra-EEC trade barriers are those which evidenced the greatest response to the establishment of a customs union. Nevertheless, no generalization can be made for all commodities, since the behavior of trade in individual goods is dependent upon a great many factors other than the effects of the Common Market.

In order to amplify the data in Table 30, it is useful to analyze change in supply and absorption shares in the case of trade in those commodities which were identified above as having in all probability been affected by the EEC. This analysis is similar to the one carried out earlier for broad commodity groups and is directed at the same questions. Is there any evidence that the "dominant" supplier country of a given commodity strengthened its position after the formation of the EEC with respect to its share of total intra-EEC trade? Moreover, did the absorption of those countries having relatively small shares in 1954 and 1958 increase rapidly after the formation of the EEC?

Drawing on the results of the analysis of broad commodity groups, we would expect the dominant supplier country of each commodity to lose part of its position to the remaining member countries. In order for any country to assume the position of dominant supplier in trade between the present Common Market countries in 1954, its producers must have been faced with moderate tariffs on the part of the remaining nations. After 1958, when tariffs began to be lowered throughout the EEC, the other countries should have begun to widen their respective supply shares. In contrast, we would expect the dominant (low tariff) importer to lose its position gradually after 1958, as the import duties of the high-tariff countries fall more than its own, in accordance with the EEC internal trade liberalization program.

Table 30

Change in the Direction of EEC Trade in 12 Selected Commodities, 1954-63[15]

Exports:* Commodity (Code)	(1) 1958 Share of EEC in Total Exports (1954=100)	(2) Annual Change 1954-58 (Col. 1-100/4)	(3) 1963 Share of EEC in Total Exports (1958=100)	(4) Annual Change 1958-63 (Col. 3-100/5)
046	1888	447.0	9	-18.2
122	145	11.3	120	4.0
112	133	8.3	149	9.8
266	144	11.0	179	15.8
512	110	2.5	101	0.2
665	99	-0.3	111	2.2
715	79	-5.3	186	17.2
721	109	2.3	100	0
541	143	10.8	61	- 7.8
732	89	-2.8	196	19.2
851	111	2.8	182	16.4
821	135	8.8	176	15.2

Table 30, Continued

Imports:* Commodity (Code)	(1) 1958 Share of EEC in Total Imports (1954=100)	(2) Annual Change 1954-58 (Col. 1-100/4)	(3) 1963 Share of EEC in Total Imports (1958=100)	(4) Annual Change 1958-63 (Col. 1-100/5
046	2583	620.8	39	-12.2
122	137	9.3	133	6.6
112	102	0.5	200	40.0
266	138	9.5	131	2.6
512	83	- 4.3	101	0.2
665	97	- 0.8	111	2.2
715	145	11.3	98	- 0.4
721	104	1.0	101	0.2
541	182	20.5	73	- 5.4
732	132	8.0	104	0.8
851	104	1.0	105	1.0
821	87	- 3.3	105	1.0

* SITC Commodity Code:

046	Wheat flours and meal	715	Metalworking machinery
122	Manufactured tobacco	721	Electric power equipment, switchgear, etc.
112	Alcoholic beverages	541	Drugs
266	Synthetic fibers	532	Road motor vehicles
512	Organic chemicals	851	Footwear
665	Glassware	821	Furniture

Table 31

Percentage of Intra-EEC Trade in Selected Commodities Supplied and Absorbed by Member Countries, 1954, 1958, and 1963[16]

Commodity	Belg.-Lux.		France		Germany		Italy		Netherlands	
	Suppl.	Abs.	Suppl.	Abs.	Suppl.	Abs.	Suppl.	Abs.	Suppl.	Abs.
Alcoholic beverages										
1954	14.3	17.5	63.6	2.8	5.9	75.6*	27.6	0.8	14.3	3.3
1958	4.4	15.6	40.2	5.1	8.4	72.1*	43.8	1.2	3.5	6.0
1963	11.2	13.4	63.5	9.0	7.8	67.9*	13.6	2.5	5.9	7.1
Synthetic fibers										
1954	19.5	39.3*	2.9	5.4	52.9	15.7	6.2	2.5	18.9	37.1
1958	16.7	24.9*	4.8	16.5	64.9	7.6	4.5	19.5	9.5	31.5
1963	8.3	35.2*	16.4	21.5	52.2	7.0	4.7	22.0	18.3	14.3
Organic chemicals										
1954	12.9	14.6	14.5	24.9	59.4	10.9	28.3	31.7*	10.4	17.9
1958	9.6	12.5	11.4	24.3	49.1	22.6	10.8	20.9*	19.2	19.8
1963	11.2	12.1	19.5	21.7	39.0	34.1	14.3	14.9*	16.0	17.2
Glassware										
1954	24.0	27.8	20.8	2.7	44.8	1.0	3.7	15.3	10.1	53.1*
1958	27.8	20.4	21.0	3.4	38.2	15.1	2.7	10.9	10.3	50.2*
1963	30.0	16.5	21.9	9.2	35.5	21.1	8.1	13.0	4.4	40.3*

Table 31, Continued

Commodity	Belg.-Lux. Suppl.	Belg.-Lux. Abs.	France Suppl.	France Abs.	Germany Suppl.	Germany Abs.	Italy Suppl.	Italy Abs.	Netherlands Suppl.	Netherlands Abs.
Metalworking machinery										
1954	9.2	14.1	6.7	35.8*	77.9	6.7	3.9	26.5	2.4	19.1
1958	12.5	12.1	6.2	43.6*	70.3	11.2	6.2	16.7	4.8	16.5
1963	13.4	17.8	13.1	31.3*	65.3	14.2	5.4	27.3	2.8	9.4
Road motor vehicles										
1954	15.0	42.5	14.2	4.1	60.4	4.5	5.7	4.5	4.6	44.4*
1958	15.7	44.1	17.7	4.0	44.5	18.4	17.4	2.6	4.7	30.9*
1963	11.5	27.1	23.0	15.4	48.8	14.7	13.9	18.8	2.9	24.0*
Footwear										
1954	21.7	55.8*	4.9	10.8	22.9	18.3	7.9	1.6	42.7	13.5
1958	14.9	37.2*	6.9	8.7	15.0	33.3	39.8	1.4	23.4	19.4
1963	10.8	19.4*	23.5	9.3	5.4	53.3	49.9	0.7	10.4	17.3
Furniture										
1954	4.4	60.1*	4.0	15.3	56.5	3.2	0.9	2.8	34.3	18.7
1958	6.4	44.1*	5.3	17.5	58.7	7.7	3.5	4.1	26.0	26.7
1963	29.7	17.4*	7.0	42.5	41.1	13.1	5.4	7.9	16.7	19.0

____ = dominant supplier * = dominant importer

The facts, given in Table 31, in general seem to support the *a priori* statements made above. In the case of all commodities with the exception of alcoholic beverages and road motor vehicles, the share of the dominant supplier declined considerably from 1958 to 1963. However, this decline in the relative position of the dominant supplier was, in most cases, already in evidence before 1958. This gives rise to the notion that supply conditions in non-dominant countries were improving over the entire 1954-63 time period, and that this enabled these countries to compete more effectively in the EEC market and hence to enhance their respective supply shares. Still, in several cases (furniture, footwear, synthetic fibers) the deterioration of the dominant supplier's share was considerably more pronounced during 1958-63 than during 1954-58, even on an annual basis. In the case of alcoholic beverages and automobiles, supply conditions favoring France and Germany, respectively, seem to have outweighed any possible Common Market effect.

On the import side the facts are in accord with theory. Dominant importers were in all cases countries with relatively low tariffs on the goods concerned. These countries lost in relative absorption to those countries whose tariffs fell more substantially after 1958. Still, in almost all cases the deterioration of the dominant importers' positions was already under way *before* the EEC was formed, and hence the impact of the Common Market itself is by no means certain. In the case of synthetic fibers, the dominant importer, Belgium-Luxembourg, lost from 1954 to 1958 and gained from 1958 to 1963; again, this cannot be explained by the formation of the EEC.

A glance at those countries which absorbed the smallest portion of intra-area trade in 1954, however, will show that in each case the country's share of total intra-imports rose considerably from 1958 to 1963 and, in most cases, also from 1954 to 1958.

SUMMARY

The analyses of the patterns and growth of intra-EEC trade, in terms both of broad commodity groups and selected individual commodities, have, in general, supported the analysis of changes evident in total trade, presented in Chapter 5.

Analysis of the growth of trade by broad commodity groups showed that total intra-EEC trade growth during the 1958-63 period was attributable largely to the expansion of trade in those commodity groups most likely to be affected by the EEC. Moreover, the commodity composition of intra-area trade changed in favor of these groups of commodities, particularly machinery and transport equipment. The rate of trade growth during the post-EEC period was highest for those commodity groups identified as probably reflecting the influence of the EEC to a considerable extent and least for those not affected by the EEC. Comparison of the rates of commodity trade growth for the pre-EEC and post-EEC periods showed that the effect of the Common Market was most pronounced in the case of machinery and transport equipment.

It was also shown that the commodity composition of intra-EEC trade changed from 1958 to 1963 substantially in favor of these same commodity groups. At the same time, an analysis of changes of supply and absorption in intra-area trade showed that the behavior of import shares substantiated the theoretical indications. On the supply side, in contrast, the behavior of export shares seems to go counter to the a priori analysis, if it is assumed that the dominant supplier of a given commodity group in pre-EEC intra-area trade was in fact the most efficient supplier. In virtually every case, the dominant supplier's position deteriorated in favor of other member countries, and a generally broader distribution of exports was evident in intra-area trade. Yet the above assumption may not be justified, and the reason for the dominant supplier's position in intra-area trade prior to the Common Market may have rested on the relative tariffs of the remaining member countries favoring the country in question. On the other hand, independent changes in supply conditions may have been stronger than the effects of the EEC tariff reductions; however, this is unlikely to be the case for virtually all commodity groups.

Essentially the same changes in the rates of trade growth, the direction of trade, and supply-absorption relationships were evident when the analysis was narrowed to individual commodities.

On balance, the findings contained in this chapter support the hypothesis suggested by the theory of economic integration, as well as the conclusions based on the analysis of total trade presented in Chapter 5. It is, however, necessary to determine whether these changes in the direction of trade and the rate of trade growth were in fact based on a reallocation of production within the EEC. This is the subject of Chapter 7.

Notes to Chapter 6

1. This code key will be repeated whenever related tables are presented below. Source: U.N., Statistical Office, Statistical Papers, Series D (New York: United Nations), 1953-65 inclusive.

2. Unfortunately, all of these analyses must be pursued in terms of current prices, since there are no adequate series available for the commodity groups under consideration. This is made amply clear in Appendix Table 16.

3. Data: Appendix Tables 13 and 14.

4. Based on data, in current prices, from Appendix Tables 13 and 14.

5. See Staffan B. Linder, An Essay on Trade and Transformation (Stockholm: Almquist and Wicksell, 1961).

6. Data: Calculated from Appendix Tables 14 and 3.

7. Based on data, in current prices, presented in Appendix Tables 13 and 14.

8. Data: Table 21 and Appendix Tables 13 and 14.

9. Data: Appendix Tables 13, 14, 3, and 4.

10. See L. B. Krause, "The European Economic Community and the U. S. Balance of Payments," Chapter 4 of Walter S. Salant, et al., The United States Balance of Payments in 1968 (Washington, D.C.: The Brookings Institution, 1963), p. 101.

11. Original SITC classification used in data for 1954 and 1958, and revised classification for 1963. Revision here affects only SITC 721, which is adjusted accordingly.

12. See Hans-Broder Krohn and Guenther Schmitt, "The Common Agricultural Policy" in Henry K. Junckersdorff (ed.), International Manual on the European Community (St. Louis: St. Louis University Press, 1963).

13. Data: Initial tariff levels from Francis K. Topping, "Comparative Tariffs and Trade," Supplementary Paper No. 14 (New York: Committee for Economic Development, 1963), Vols. I and II. Commodity Trade Statistics, from United Nations, Secretariat, Statistical Office, Statistical Papers, Series D, 1954, 1958, and 1963 (New York: United Nations).

14. Data: United Nations, Secretariat, Statistical Office, Statistical Papers, Series D, 1954, 1958, and 1963 (New York: United Nations).

15. Ibid.

16. Ibid.

CHAPTER 7 CHANGE IN THE PATTERN OF PRODUCTION IN THE COMMON MARKET

The preceding two chapters analyzed changes which occurred in the direction of trade, as well as the growth of trade, during the first six years after the European Economic Community was formed. This was done, both in aggregate terms and by means of a commodity-by-commodity breakdown of trade, in order to determine whether there was any meaningful evidence that the EEC did, in fact, influence trade growth and the direction of intra-EEC trade roughly in accordance with the predictions of the theory of economic integration.

However, changes in trade patterns and the rate of trade growth are in part a manifestation of a more fundamental change in the economic structure of the community: the geographical reallocation of production. Chapter 3 outlined the changes in the locus of production within the EEC which the theory of economic integration anticipates. Briefly, the removal of internal barriers to trade and competition causes consumers or users in the member states to purchase from the lowest-cost supplier within the community as a whole. If a community supplier is more efficient than the domestic supplier, purchases would shift from the latter to the former and the pattern of production for the commodity in question would shift from one EEC country in favor of another.

Similarly, if the lowest-cost pre-EEC supplier were situated outside the community, and if the removal of internal tariffs and the movement toward a common external tariff changed prices in such a way as to render a less efficient EEC supplier the lowest-cost producer, purchases would shift accordingly. Again, the most efficient EEC supplier's output would rise, this time at the expense of the external producer. In the latter case, the importance of the most efficient supplier country's national output, relative to total EEC output of the commodity in question, would rise and there would appear a geographical shift in the locus of production within the community.

These changes in the patterns of production would be reflected in the form of intra-EEC trade growth and changes in the direction of trade, as analyzed in the preceding two chapters. This chapter attempts to determine what changes occurred in the locus of production directly, insofar as data availability permits. Unquestionably, production cost factors are not the only consideration involved; rather, tastes and quality aspects may also be of considerable importance.

TOTAL INDUSTRIAL PRODUCTION

Before going into an analysis of changes in the pattern of output of selected commodities for which the relevant data is available, it may be of interest to determine what happened to EEC industrial output, in general, from 1958 to 1963 and to compare changes in the locus of EEC industrial production during this period with that evidenced during the earlier, 1953-58 period.

As Table 32 below shows, in 1953 France contributed the largest part of the industrial production of the six present EEC countries combined. Germany was considerably behind with 35 per cent of total output. By 1958 this relationship had been reversed, with Germany contributing 41. 6 per cent of industrial production and the French dropping to 34. 3 per cent. The rise of the German share was most striking during this period, and Italy also gained to some degree. The German and Italian gains in relative industrial production were made almost entirely at the expense of France, with the Netherlands' share remaining constant and Belgium-Luxembourg declining somewhat.

This trend in the changing relative importance of industrial output, evidenced during the 1953-58 period, continued in substantially the same manner during the post-EEC, 1958-63 period. Again, Germany and Italy gained at the expense of France and Belgium-Luxembourg, with the Netherlands gaining only slightly. This time it was the Italian relative position which benefited most significantly, in line with the high rate of that country's economic growth during the 1958-63 period.

There is little evidence of an effect of the Common

Market here, and the entire period seems to be characterized by German and Italian gains in relative importance in EEC industrial production at the expense of France.

Table 32

Percentage of Total EEC Industrial Production at 1958 Factor Cost Supplied by Member Countries[1]

	Belg.-Lux.	France	Germany	Italy	Netherlands
1953	5.9	41.9	35.0	12.4	4.8
Change	- 0.4	- 7.6	+ 6.6	+ 1.4	0
1958	5.5	34.3	41.6	13.8	4.8
Change	- 0.5	- 2.8	+ 0.4	+ 2.7	+0.1
1963	5.0	31.5	42.0	16.5	4.9

But this is not a true indication of the geographical reallocation of production in the Common Market. A substantial part of the industrial production of the member countries is exported to nations outside the EEC, and expansion of such exports has little to do with the movement toward economic union within the Common Market. What is needed is a share analysis of the entire non-import EEC market for industrial products. That is, what percentage of the total EEC market for industrial goods was held by each member country?

A given member nation's absorption of industrial products is supplied from three different sources: 1) domestic production, 2) imports from the EEC, and 3) imports from non-member countries.

For example, if France's producers were highly inefficient in the face of declining intra-EEC tariffs in 1958, we would expect domestic production to be reduced and replaced by imports from the remaining EEC countries. In addition, if movement toward the EEC common external tariff meant lower French duties on imports from third countries, part of French output might also be supplanted by imports from non-member countries; the latter effect, however, would probably be far smaller than the intra-EEC effect, since the tariff reductions on imports from third countries would in any event be far smaller. In contrast, if the arithmetic-average principle (explained in Chapter 2) used in determining the EEC common external tariff dictated a rise in French duties on extra-EEC imports, the effect on production patterns within the Common Market would be correspondingly greater.

Since we are interested here primarily in shifts in production patterns within the EEC in response to the formation of the Common Market--not shifts in patterns of total production--we will concentrate on changes in the locus of industrial production among the EEC member nations. For any one country, this necessitates an analysis of change in domestic output both consumed or used domestically and exported to the remainder of the EEC, in relation to total EEC output consumed or used within the Common Market. Such an analysis would yield the internal market share held by that country and may be done for each EEC member nation for any year for which the necessary data are available. In this case, it would be useful to make such an analysis for 1953, 1958, and 1963 in order to observe any changes in the relative shares of the member countries which may have taken place. As a general framework for such an analysis, both in the case of total industrial production and for individual commodities, we may use the following relations:

For any EEC member country during a given year let:

AP_i = total industrial production at factor cost,
AE_i = total exports of industrial products to non-EEC nations;

therefore:

$(AP_i - AE_i)$ = industrial output consumed or used in the EEC (i.e., domestically and exported to rest of EEC);

and: $\sum_{1}^{5}(AP_i - AE_i)$ = total EEC industrial production for the specified year which is consumed or used in the EEC;[2]

hence:

$$\frac{(AP_i - AE_i)}{\sum_{1}^{5}(AP_i - AE_i)}$$ = proportion of the total non-import market for industrial goods supplied by a given member nation.

Clearly, this method may be applied equally to individual commodities, commodity groups, and total industrial production. Decline in one country's relative competitiveness during the period between two given years should appear as a lower share rate, as domestic output is partly supplanted by imports from the EEC, and as that country's exports to the remainder of the EEC decline in relative importance.

Table 33 presents these relative market shares for the EEC member countries for the years 1953, 1958, and 1963, and compares them with the respective over-all industrial production shares computed in Table 32 above.

Table 33

Relative EEC Market and Total Industrial Production Shares, Common Market Countries, 1953, 1958, and 1963[3]
(per cent of total)

	1953		1958		1963	
Country	Market	Output	Market	Output	Market	Output
Belg.-Lux.	6.3	5.9	5.7	5.5	5.4	5.0
France	41.7	41.9	35.5	34.3	33.8	31.5
Germany	34.0	35.0	39.0	41.6	39.1	42.0
Italy	12.5	12.4	14.5	13.8	16.1	16.5
Netherlands	5.5	4.8	5.7	4.8	5.6	4.9

It is evident that the respective EEC countries' market shares for industrial products correspond closely to their corresponding shares of total industrial production. Just as in the case of industrial output, France lost considerably from 1953 to 1958 and from 1958 to 1963, which was also true to a far smaller degree in the case of Belgium-Luxembourg. The French and BLEU losses were taken over by Germany and Italy; the Netherlands retained an approximately constant share of the total EEC market for industrial products throughout.

It is interesting that the French and BLEU relative losses as well as the German and Italian gains in each case were considerably more pronounced during 1953-58 than during 1958-63. This is certainly contrary to our expectations, which anticipated a considerably more pronounced reallocation of industrial production after the formation of the EEC than during the pre-Common Market period. This would seem to suggest that, on an aggregate level, factors other than economic integration (i.e., those forces which caused the observed geographical redistribution of industrial output during 1953-58) were of determining importance, and that these factors were operating in the same direction during both periods, though less strongly during the latter period.

From this highly aggregative picture, then, little can be said about the impact of the Common Market on the locus of industrial production. It may very well be that changes in the locus of production of various goods categories were mutually offsetting, so that little change resulted in total industrial production. Indeed, this is what would be expected if increased geographical specialization were to have occurred among the EEC countries in the production of goods categories subsumed under the general heading of industrial production.

SELECTED COMMODITIES

It is far more likely that the anticipated shifts in the locus of production would show up in the case of individual goods, especially where cost and price considerations are of determining importance. Hence, this section will present an analysis of reallocation of production, similar to that given above, for selected commodities. An attempt is made to select a broad range of commodities, representative of all aspects of industrial production in the EEC. However, this attempt is not altogether successful due to a lack of availability and continuity of the required data over the entire period under consideration.[4]

It will be possible to gain a broad insight into changes in the patterns of production for a variety of commodities within the EEC by analyzing the raw production figures and each EEC country's relative contribution to total Common Market output. Such an analysis, of course, does not purport to isolate the "EEC effect." The latter relates only to shifts occurring in the locus of production which are attributable to the removal of barriers to (1) internal mobility of goods and (2) the factors of production. The data on over-all production patterns combine this factor with the expansion of internal demand (which might also be attributed in part to the EEC) and the growth of production of exports to countries outside the Common Market, which are largely independent of developments within the community.

Table 34 below presents an analysis of this type for twenty commodities: primary aluminum, wool fabrics, cotton fabrics, rayon and acetate filament yarn, rayon and acetate staple, agricultural tractors, automobiles, commercial vehicles, nitrogenous fertilizers, canned fish, sugar, margarine, beer, newsprint, sulphuric acid, zinc, cement, superphosphates, fish meal, and cheese. All of these commodities were subject to the EEC internal trade liberalization program and thus can be expected to reflect its influence to the extent that the quantity demanded is sensitive to changes in price.

A glance at the list of commodities will show that the price-elasticity of demand may be expected to vary substantially over the range of goods presented. It might be fairly high, for example, in the case of such homogeneous goods as primary aluminum, rayon and acetate staple, and zinc; and fairly low for commercial vehicles, agricultural tractors, and automobiles. At the same time, it must be remembered that high transport costs relative to price may effectively prevent trade, despite tariff reductions, in such goods as cement. Finally, output of certain commodities such as canned fish and sugar are subject to non-economic considerations which will affect the member nations' relative output shares during the years given here. This could be remedied only by the presentation and analysis of time series data.

Most of these commodities were produced in each of the Common Market countries during the entire period under consideration, thereby providing a good opportunity for observing changes in the locus of production. However, an output share analysis for a given commodity clearly may be made even if each EEC country does not produce that commodity, and hence this condition is not an essential requirement for such an analysis.

Table 34

Percentage of Total EEC Output of Selected Commodities Supplied by Member Countries [5]

Commodity	Year	Benelux	France	Germany	Italy	Average Pre-EEC Duty (%)
Primary aluminum	1953	0	39.1	42.1	18.8	
	1958	0	45.7	37.0	17.3	8.6
	1963	0	49.8	34.9	15.3	
Wool fabrics	1953	15.4	27.9	25.7	31.1	
	1958	14.9	29.9	24.9	30.4	16.6
	1963	16.2	30.1	22.3	31.4	
Cotton fabrics	1953	1.1	32.8	39.1	17.4	
	1958	1.0	34.0	39.7	16.6	16.0
	1963	1.2	32.0	36.8	19.7	
Rayon and acetate filament yarn	1953	18.8	24.5	27.5	29.1	
	1958	18.6	25.1	28.9	27.4	15.0
	1963	21.4	21.5	28.9	32.6	
Rayon and acetate staple	1953	11.3	19.3	47.0	22.3	
	1958	9.2	23.0	43.8	24.0	12.7
	1963	9.4	20.5	43.9	26.2	
Agricultural tractors	1953	0	23.8	66.2	10.0	
	1958	0	37.7	54.3	8.1	19.8
	1963	0	32.4	50.8	16.8	
Automobiles	1953	7.9	35.5	41.3	15.3	
	1958	5.3	35.2	45.0	14.5	28.7
	1963	5.9	28.8	43.3	21.9	
Commercial vehicles	1953	4.2	44.2	43.8	7.8	
	1958	3.4	36.4	55.7	4.5	28.7
	1963	3.6	30.3	57.0	9.1	
Nitrogenous fertilizers	1953	27.7	22.1	37.4	12.8	
	1958	24.5	19.6	40.2	15.7	1.6
	1963	21.0	22.3	35.0	21.7	

(continued)

Table 34, Continued

Commodity	Year	Bene-lux	France	Germany	Italy	Average Pre-EEC Duty (%)
Canned fish	1953	9.6	39.2	51.2	0	
	1958	8.1	30.2	50.9	10.8	24.4
	1963	10.2	41.7	23.0	25.1	
Sugar	1953	21.2	26.5	33.7	18.6	
	1958	18.9	28.6	32.2	20.4	80.0
	1963	16.3	34.2	28.8	20.7	
Margarine	1953	30.2	8.3	61.6	0	
	1958	31.8	9.6	58.6	0	25.0
	1963	35.6	12.1	52.3	0	
Beer	1953	24.7	17.2	54.8	3.2	
	1958	17.6	23.6	56.7	2.2	30.0
	1963	15.5	17.6	63.2	3.6	
Newsprint	1953	18.8	42.0	24.9	14.3	
	1958	20.1	39.5	22.8	17.5	14.7
	1963	19.5	33.9	17.8	28.9	
Sulphuric acid	1953	22.4	19.6	31.5	26.6	
	1958	21.4	20.8	34.0	23.7	4.0
	1963	19.4	23.1	31.3	26.2	
Zinc	1953	40.8	17.5	31.1	10.6	
	1958	35.3	26.2	28.1	10.4	5.8
	1963	33.4	28.4	26.8	11.3	
Cement	1953	14.6	24.5	40.1	20.8	
	1958	10.5	26.4	38.2	24.9	8.0
	1963	9.9	26.2	42.4	32.0	
Super-phosphates	1953	19.1	24.6	9.9	46.4	
	1958	24.4	26.8	9.4	39.3	4.4
	1963	26.4	35.2	6.2	32.3	
Fish meal	1953	20.2	18.8	61.0	0	
	1958	10.0	9.9	74.9	0	4.9
	1963	8.3	15.9	75.9	0	

Table 34, Continued

Commodity	Year	Bene-lux	France	Germany	Italy	Average Pre-EEC Duty (%)
Cheese	1953	18.2	32.2	17.7	31.8	
	1958	16.7	35.1	22.0	26.2	23.0
	1963	19.6	31.5	22.9	26.0	

The pattern of industrial production, as reflected in Table 34 above, shows some interesting characteristics. First, in almost all cases, the dominant producer in 1958 either lost its position to another country or declined in the relative importance of its output by 1963. This means that there was no observable trend toward specialization in production during that period; rather, a movement is evident away from specialization toward a more even distribution of output throughout the community. It is similar to the developments observed in the case of total industrial output earlier in this chapter. One notable exception is the production of beer, with Germany strengthening its relative position considerably between 1958 and 1963 (a more pronounced continuation of a movement already in evidence between 1953 and 1958). However, this may be a case where demand considerations are of overwhelming importance and favored Germany over all other EEC member countries.

As was mentioned earlier, this analysis of relative output of a variety of goods cannot hope to isolate the EEC effect. Aside from exports to non-EEC countries, it is affected by differential rates of GNP growth and other factors not explicitly associated with the development of a free trade area. Exports to third countries may be eliminated by means of an analysis similar to that presented earlier in connection with total industrial production. That is, for any one EEC country let:

AP_i = total national output of commodity i in year A;

AE_i = total exports of commodity i to non-EEC countries in year A;

hence: $(AP_i - AE_i)$ = production of commodity i which is consumed or used in the EEC, i.e., the contribution of this country to total EEC output of commodity i which is consumed <u>within</u> the EEC;

and: $\sum_{1}^{5}(AP_i - AE_i)$ = total EEC output of commodity i which is consumed within the EEC; [6]

hence: $\dfrac{(AP_i - AE_i)}{\sum_{1}^{5}(AP_i - AE_i)}$ = proportion of total non-import EEC market for commodity i during year A which is supplied by a given member nation.

These proportions may then be compared for the years 1958, 1963, and, where possible, 1953, for each commodity under consideration. The effect of exports to third countries on national output is thus eliminated. If this analysis follows the same pattern as the relative national contributions to EEC industrial production presented in Table 34, for a more limited range of goods, then it will be possible to say that the percentage of total output supplied by a member country is a fairly good approximation of the locus of intra-EEC production. The relevant data for five commodities for the years 1953, 1958, and 1963 are presented in Table 35 below: cheese, canned fish, margarine, cement, and zinc.

It is clear that the most substantial shifts in the locus of production for the EEC market occurred in the high-tariff commodities, from 1958 to 1963. In the case of canned fish, Germany lost over half the market to her Common Market partners, primarily France and Italy, while there was no such development prior to the formation of the EEC. Similarly, in the production of margarine, Germany lost to France and the Benelux countries (predominantly to the Netherlands), although it still remained the dominant supplier of this commodity.

Change in the locus of production was far less pronounced in the case of cheese, with the Benelux countries and Germany gaining slightly in EEC market share at the expense of France and Italy. An explanation for this might be found in the highly differentiated nature of the individual nations' cheese output, and the possibly low price elasticity of demand resulting therefrom. However, this idea is refuted by the export data (Appendix Table 18) which shows an enormous increase in intra-EEC trade in cheese. Hence the "consumption effect" (see Chapter 3) must have been far more important than the "production effect," resulting in a great increase in the volume of trade as a result of the EEC but little or no change in the locus of production.

Table 35

Proportion of Total Non-Import EEC Market for Selected Commodities Supplied by Member Countries, 1953, 1958, and 1963 (per cent)[7]

Commodity	Year	Benelux	France	Germany	Italy	Pre-EEC Mean Duty*
Cheese	1953	15.9	32.6	18.9	32.5	
(metric	1958	15.5	35.1	23.3	26.2	23.0
tons)	1963	17.8	32.1	24.1	26.0	
Canned	1953	8.0	39.3	51.8	0.9	
fish (met-	1958	6.4	29.8	52.4	11.3	24.4
ric tons)	1963	8.4	43.1	22.0	26.4	
Margarine	1953	27.7	7.0	65.4	0	
(metric	1958	25.7	7.9	66.4	0	25.0
tons)	1963	33.1	12.3	54.6	0	
Cement	1953	10.2	25.0	41.2	23.6	
(metric	1958	7.9	26.2	39.6	26.2	8.0
tons)	1963	8.6	23.2	39.0	29.2	
Zinc	1953	33.7	26.8	38.7	9.6	
(metric	1958	26.3	32.5	30.2	11.0	5.8
tons)	1963	28.2	32.1	26.7	13.0	

* In per cent *ad valorem*. Tariff on cheese was changed to a specific duty under the EEC common agricultural policy, with all quantitative restrictions eliminated in 1959, in accordance with the "variable levy" system. As a result, trade liberalization during the 1958-63 period was not as substantial as it would otherwise have been. See "General Agreement on Tariffs and Trade," *Trade in Agriculture Products* (Geneva: GATT, 1965), pp. 3-25.

In the case of cement, there was little change in the locus of production, although Italy gained somewhat in its market share, primarily at the expense of France. The reason might be found in the relatively low initial tariff applied to this good--and the resulting small extent of duty reductions which are possible--as well as the high cost of transport of cement relative to its value. Zinc showed a similar pattern, with Benelux and Italy gaining. The substantial increase in intra-EEC trade again suggests a consumption effect of significantly more importance than the reallocation of production.

In general, there is no marked trend toward specialization of production evident from the data presented on these five goods. In fact, the reverse was true, with a decrease in the relative importance of the dominant supplier in each case and a more generalized distribution of market shares occurring over the entire period. This development was, however, accompanied by a marked increase in the volume of trade in each commodity within the EEC.

It would be difficult and premature to make general conclusions regarding shifts in the locus of production, or the lack thereof, from the few commodities examined above. Table 36 below presents similar data for nine additional commodity groups for the years 1958 and 1963 which may be more representative of over-all industrial output. Unfortunately, incomparability and the lack of availability of data for 1953 made it impossible to compute figures for that year. Hence it is not possible to make a comparison of changes which occurred during the 1953-58 period with those for 1958-63.

Again, in the majority of cases the market share of the dominant supplier declined from 1958 to 1963, thus coinciding with the findings presented earlier in the chapter. As a result, very little increased specialization is evident and the reverse seems to be the case. Notable exceptions are beer and commercial vehicles, where Germany increased its share of the EEC market and strengthened its position as dominant supplier. In addition, it should be noted that sugar came under the EEC agricultural regulations and hence did not undergo extensive trade liberalization.

The Benelux countries gained substantially in the case of wool and cotton fabrics and synthetic fibers, while Italy increased its market share most noticeably in the case of

Table 36

Proportion of Total Non-Import EEC Market for Selected Commodities Supplied by Member Countries, 1958 and 1963 (per cent)[8]

Commodity	Year	Benelux	France	Germany	Italy	Mean Pre-EEC Duty*
Wool fabrics (metric tons)	1958	14.6	32.5	27.4	25.5	16.6
	1963	17.5	33.1	24.4	25.0	
Cotton fabrics (metric tons)	1958	25.6	27.6	33.2	13.5	16.0
	1963	31.5	23.8	28.9	15.8	
Rayon and acetate fiber yarn (metric tons)	1958	15.8	27.2	31.4	25.6	15.0
	1963	21.4	22.2	27.8	28.6	
Agricultural tractors (units)	1958	8.7	35.7	53.4	10.2	19.8
	1963	11.6	33.2	50.8	14.8	
Automobiles (units)	1958	7.1	35.1	37.4	20.5	28.7
	1963	6.9	31.8	35.2	26.1	
Commercial vehicles (units)	1958	4.1	37.9	53.4	4.6	28.7
	1963	3.9	31.1	56.1	8.9	
Beer (hectoliters)	1958	17.6	21.0	59.0	2.3	30.0
	1963	15.3	17.6	63.6	3.7	
Sugar (metric tons)	1958	18.6	22.7	36.1	22.7	80.0
	1963	17.5	25.0	33.5	24.1	
Newsprint (metric tons)	1958	19.5	39.7	23.2	17.7	14.7
	1963	19.4	33.9	17.9	28.8	

* See note to Table 35.

agricultural tractors, road motor vehicles, and newsprint. France lost in relative position in every commodity except sugar, while Germany gained only in beer and commercial vehicles. Thus the changes in relative market shares for the commodities selected seem to show decreased concentration of output, with the smaller EEC members gaining at the expense of the larger ones. It should also be noted that these figures closely parallel the related data on production, presented in Table 33 above. This implies that exports to non-EEC countries were not of determining importance, and that the industrial output figures may be used as a reasonably accurate proxy for the locus of production within the Common Market.

Comparison of the changes in market shares with the corresponding data on the volume of trade (Appendix Table 19) seems to show that the growth of intra-EEC trade was not a reflection of changes in the locus of production (the "production effect" of economic integration), but rather changes in demand patterns, i. e., the "consumption effect." For instance, if all EEC countries' output of automobiles grew at about the same rate there would be little change in their relative market shares or their relative contributions to total EEC auto production. Yet at the same time, intra-EEC trade in automobiles might grow enormously as a result of internal tariff reductions, with both German exports of cars to France and French exports of cars to Germany increasing substantially, and so forth. In this case there would be no change in the locus of production, yet a considerable growth of internal trade; each nation would simply export a larger share of its output to its EEC partners.

EXPORTS AND TOTAL OUTPUT

If this were in fact the case, we would expect to find that the ratio of intra-EEC exports to total output increased during the 1958-63 period for most commodities under consideration here. The same statement could also be made of total industrial production. The relevant data are presented in Table 37 below.

Over-all industrial production certainly behaved in the manner indicated. For each EEC economic area, a far greater proportion of industrial production was exported to the

Common Market in 1963 than in 1958. In fact, for the Benelux, the intra-area exports exceeded half the total industrial output. While the increase in importance of the EEC as a market for exports was already in evidence in the case of Benelux from 1953 to 1958, this was not true for the other Common Market nations. German, French, and Italian exports to the EEC grew only slightly from 1953 to 1958 as a proportion of total national industrial output but rose very sharply from 1958 to 1963: In the case of France and Italy, they almost doubled during this period.

Since this phenomenon is evident in the case of all EEC nations, we cannot speak of a general reallocation of over-all industrial production within the EEC: Had there been such a general shift in the locus of production, the intra-area export shares relative to total output would have declined in the case of the less competitive countries, which they did not.

Table 37

Percentage of Total Output of Selected Commodities Exported to EEC, 1958 and 1963[9]

Commodity	Year	Benelux	France	Germany	Italy
Canned fish	1953	17.2	0.3	0.9	1.7
	1958	23.1	0.1	1.7	0.7
	1963	40.5	0.6	3.5	0.5
Cheese	1953	33.4	0.4	2.1	0.8
	1958	36.0	0.7	2.6	1.2
	1963	30.6	6.5	5.2	1.3
Margarine	1953	22.6	1.5	0.6	0
	1958	3.5	8.6	0.1	0
	1963	3.8	0.2	0.2	0
Cement	1953	5.4	1.1	0.5	0
	1958	22.2	5.6	4.9	0.1
	1963	13.4	1.9	2.1	0
Zinc	1953	25.2	0	6.5	3.0
	1958	32.3	0.1	5.4	5.1
	1963	40.6	6.5	4.3	0

(continued)

Table 37, Continued

Commodity	Year	Benelux	France	Germany	Italy
Beer	1953	-	-	-	-
	1958	0.9	0.1	1.1	0
	1963	4.7	0.5	0.6	0
Sugar	1953	-	-	-	-
	1958	1.6	0.6	0	0
	1963	2.2	13.7	0.2	1.0
Wool fabrics	1953	-	-	-	-
	1958	20.1	1.9	1.7	18.0
	1963	17.4	4.6	2.3	26.4
Cotton fabrics	1953	-	-	-	-
	1958	6.1	0.8	1.1	1.2
	1963	11.3	5.7	2.9	1.0
Rayon and acetate yarn	1953	-	-	-	-
	1958	25.1	0.9	2.9	3.4
	1963	38.7	13.1	15.6	14.5
Agricultural tractors	1953	-	-	-	-
	1958	14.0	37.2	10.4	0
	1963	23.5	8.4	17.3	13.3
Automobiles	1953	-	-	-	-
	1958	35.5	5.3	6.6	2.1
	1963	42.2	19.8	20.1	13.0
Commercial vehicles	1953	-	-	-	-
	1958	14.1	1.3	4.8	0.8
	1963	31.8	6.3	9.2	10.6
Newsprint	1953	-	-	-	-
	1958	33.0	0	0.3	0.3
	1963	32.3	1.2	1.4	0.1
Total industrial production	1953	32.8	4.6	9.1	4.0
	1958	45.2	5.8	10.7	6.9
	1963	51.6	10.6	16.8	13.6

In the case of the individual commodities presented in Table 37, similar conclusions may be drawn. An increasing percentage of total output exported to the EEC seemed to be a general characteristic, apparent in a wide variety of commodities and for the several countries involved. If there had been considerable reallocation of the production of a given good within the Common Market, we would expect the proportion of intra-EEC exports to rise relative to total output in one or two countries and decline in the rest. That is, the lowest-cost suppliers would take over part or all of the markets of the high-cost producers. However, we also observe an increasing proportion of total output of certain commodities being exported to the EEC on the part of a number of countries and sometimes on the part of all member nations.

For example, in the case of rayon and acetate yarn, commercial vehicles, automobiles, and sugar, each EEC member increased in the share of intra-area exports relative to total output. Similarly, in the case of canned fish, cheese, margarine, wool and cotton fabrics, and agricultural tractors three out of four EEC areas increased intra-exports relative to total output. This indicates a substantial amount of cross-trading of commodities with the member countries exporting and importing the same commodities to and from each other. There is little positive evidence of a change in the locus of production in the case of most commodities examined here. Possible exceptions are beer and zinc. In the case of cement, the export shares of each country declined, possibly due to transport costs and other supply considerations.

SUMMARY

The purpose of this chapter has been to attempt to determine the extent of changes in the locus of production within the Common Market as a result of the process of economic integration. Whereas the analysis was to some extent hindered by a lack of comparability and availability of data, certain significant observations may be noted.

First, it was noted that the proportion of total EEC industrial output contributed by each member country changed substantially during 1958-63. There was little evidence of the effect of the EEC, however, and Germany and Italy gained in relation to the rest of the EEC nations both during 1958-63 and

1953-58. This was true both of total industrial production as well as that part of industrial output consumed or used within the EEC. There was, however, little reason for expecting a marked EEC effect on the locus of total industrial output, since changes in the locus of production of individual goods would tend to offset each other, thereby leaving the over-all output shares relatively unchanged.

In the case of selected commodities, analysis of changes in relative output shares, both for total output and for output destined only for the EEC market, there was little evidence of changes in the supply patterns along the lines of the *a priori* analysis based on the theory of economic integration. In general, the dominant supplier country in the majority of cases gradually lost its position, and a more even distribution of production throughout the EEC was in evidence. The results of this analysis, rejecting the notion of widespread changes in the locus of production due to the formation of the Common Market, were supported by an analysis of the importance of intra-EEC exports relative to total output for a variety of commodities.

In spite of the apparent absence of shifts in the locus of production resulting from the formation of the EEC, it is hardly possible to assert that the Common Market had no positive effects upon productive efficiency within the union. The theory of economic integration suggests that such increases in efficiency should come from the reallocation of production from less efficient to more efficient suppliers as customs union is achieved. This appears not to have occurred in large measure in the EEC. But it can easily be shown that productive efficiency could have been enhanced even without substantial shifts in the production locus.

The gradual elimination of protective internal trade barriers within the Common Market doubtlessly increased interfirm competition from the outset. But, more importantly, it must have caused businessmen to anticipate increasingly fierce competition as tariffs gradually came down. With this in mind, it is entirely possible that higher-cost firms were able to enhance their levels of operating efficiency and thereby reduce costs, knowing full well that failure to do so would lead to their eventual demise. If this in fact occurred, then the Common Market exercised a fully beneficial force on productive efficiency without necessitating widespread shifts in production patterns.

The evidence opposing the theory predicting substantial reallocation of production stands alongside the somewhat more convincing evidence, gathered in the two previous chapters, of important increases in intra-EEC trade which probably resulted largely from the formation of the Common Market. The only possible conclusion which can be drawn from these data is that the reallocation occurred in consumption, not in production. It is, of course, possible that the commodity sample used here is not representative of all goods entering intra-EEC trade. It is equally possible that the commodity classifications are wide and therefore heterogeneous, thus permitting various changes to occur within the categories which do not appear in the aggregate. These are only two of the many factors which call for caution in interpreting the results of this analysis. Nevertheless, the high rate of trade growth does seem to reflect a broadening of consumption patterns, encompassing all of the EEC, in each member country, with considerable cross-trading of similar commodities. While there is little doubt that competition among producers situated in the member countries increased as a result of the formation of the Common Market, this does not seem to have resulted in a meaningful reallocation of production among them. The greater freedom of choice provided by the Common Market to consumers in the member countries, then, seems to have been a very real and important effect of the EEC.

Notes to Chapter 7

1. Data: Table 17 in Appendix. See also note to that table.

2. The numbers 1–5 represent the five EEC economic areas: Belgium-Luxembourg, France, Germany, Italy, and the Netherlands.

3. Data: Table 32 and Appendix Table 17.

4. The data are taken from: OEEC/OECD, General Statistics, (Paris: OEEC/OECD), various issues; United Nations, Statistical Yearbooks (New York: United Nations), various issues, 1953-65 inclusive; European Communities,

Statistical Office, Industriestatistik (Luxembourg: European Communities), various issues, 1953-65 inclusive.

5. Data: United Nations, Secretariat, Statistical Office, Statistical Yearbook (New York: United Nations), various issues, 1953-65 inclusive; OEEC/OECD, General Statistics (Paris: OEEC/OECD), various issues, 1953-65 inclusive; European Communities, Statistical Office, Industriestatistik (Luxembourg: European Communities), various issues, 1953-65 inclusive.

6. Numbers 1–5 represent the four EEC economic areas: Benelux, France, Germany, and Italy.

7. Data: Appendix Table 18. Mean tariff levels for pre-EEC years constitute the unweighted average of the five EEC tariff areas' pre-EEC import duties on the goods concerned. Source: Francis K. Topping, Atlantic Tariffs and Trade (New York: CED, 1962).

8. Data: See note to Table 35.

9. Data: Appendix Tables 18, 19, and 16.

CHAPTER 8 CONCLUSIONS

What inferences may be drawn from the empirical examination of trade and production data, as presented in the preceding three chapters, when viewed in the light of the theory of economic integration applied to the particular institutional arrangements of the European Common Market?

First, we conclude that the formation of the EEC did indeed stimulate the volume of over-all trade between the member countries to a very substantial degree. This statement is based upon the results of a number of different analytical approaches. Comparing trade growth for the periods 1953-58, 1958-63, and 1958-65 (i.e., the periods before and after the formation of the Common Market), it was found that the average annual rate of intra-area trade growth in real terms was 17.4 per cent (1958-63) and 15.6 per cent (1958-65) after the formation of the EEC, compared with 11.1 per cent during the 1953-58 period. The increase in the trade growth rate is sufficiently great to be considered significant even when viewed in the light of the various problems, outlined in Chapter 5, connected with such comparisons. In fact, the surprising increase in the rate of intra-EEC trade growth coincides with a similar phenomenon found by Verdoorn in his analysis of Benelux intra-trade growth.[1] He attributed the high growth rate to abnormally high price elasticities of demand and an increased "willingness" to trade on the part of Benelux firms. This reasoning bears some similarity to the findings presented here, which attribute the rise in the trade growth rate partly to expectations on the part of businessmen of a fully integrated Common Market, in addition to the reduction of non-tariff impediments to trade and the increasing mobility of productive factors throughout the EEC.

Moreover, it was found that there was a good correlation between the degree of intra-EEC import expansion and the extent of tariff reductions undertaken by a given member nation, although the evidence is not sufficiently strong to justify attributing the internal trade expansion <u>primarily</u> to tariff reductions. The analysis of shifts in the direction of EEC trade likewise favored the conclusion of a substantial EEC-effect. From 1953 to 1958, the percentage of EEC exports destined for the EEC rose very gradually from 28.4 to 30.5. This is to be compared with the corresponding rise from 30.5 per cent to 42.4 per cent for the post-EEC, 1958-63 period and to 43.4 per cent in 1965. The increased inward orientation of exports was paralleled by a similar, though somewhat less pronounced, trend in the case of imports. Whereas such a trend on the export side might be partly explained by a higher rate of GNP growth in the EEC than in the rest of the world, this is certainly not true on the import side, where a similar phenomenon was observed.

Moreover, this rapidly increasing inward orientation of trade evident for the EEC as a whole after 1958 also characterizes the trade of every Common Market member country. In fact, both Belgium-Luxembourg and the Netherlands sent over half their exports to, and obtained more than half of their imports from, the European Economic Community in 1963 and 1965.

Extension of the analysis of changes in the direction of EEC trade, by means of the rate of regionalization of imports and exports, showed that the movement toward inward orientation was more pronounced during the post-EEC period than during 1953-58. This was true both for total EEC trade and for the trade of the individual member countries. Most importantly, the rates of regionalization of imports were greatest for those countries which possessed the highest pre-EEC duties and hence subject to the most significant internal tariff reductions.

Combining the analyses of imports and exports by means of weighted share indexes for total trade, it was found that there must have been a substantial EEC effect. According to this analysis, the EEC effect must have been about 28.6 per cent of the weighted share, i.e., the formation of the Common Market was responsible for an increase in regionalization of total EEC trade of 28.6 per cent from 1953-58 to 1958-63. Comparison of the weighted share indexes for trade among the member countries again showed a close relationship to the degree of trade liberalization undertaken by the individual nations.

All of the factors associated with the EEC contributed to the changes in over-all trade patterns outlined above. Only the impact of income changes on intra-EEC trade was left to be explained, i.e.: Would not intra-Common Market trade have grown substantially even without the formation of the EEC, due to the high rate of economic growth in these countries? Analysis of this factor by means of a projected partial average propensity to import for each EEC country showed that a relatively large part of the intra-trade growth from 1958 to 1963 could be explained by GNP growth in the member countries. However, the results of the calculations attributed a probable value of 42.8 per cent and a minimum of 29.7 per cent of the 1958-63 intra-trade growth to factors other than GNP growth. This coincides with the earlier findings of a marked rise in intra-EEC trade growth, with very little change in the rate of GNP growth from 1953-58 to 1958-63. Again, those countries with the highest pre-EEC trade barriers apparently reacted most to the formation of the Common Market.

Analysis of price effects and the influence of economic distance showed that neither of these factors detract from the conclusion of a very substantial impact of the EEC upon the volume of trade among its members. This was supported by a comparison of intra-EEC trade growth with the expansion of trade between other groups of countries: the OECD countries (excluding the EEC), the European Free Trade Association, the developed countries (excluding the EEC), the European OECD members excluding the EEC, intra-North America, as well as world trade. Intra-EEC trade growth for 1958-63 was by far the highest, although the increase in the rate of growth from 1953-58 to 1958-63 was greater in the case of EFTA. Also, the change in the direction of EEC trade as a result of integration was considerably greater than in the case of EFTA. At the same time, intra-EEC trade grew substantially as a per cent of trade among developed countries, while the corresponding EFTA share actually declined.

This evidence in support of a substantial EEC effect on trade, presented in Chapter 5, was further substantiated by the analysis of commodity trade patterns and growth in Chapter 6. The analysis of the growth of intra-EEC trade by broad commodity groups shows that the over-all intra-area trade growth during 1958-63 was attributable largely to the expansion of trade in those commodity groups which were identified as most likely to be affected by the EEC. In addition, the commodity composition of intra-community trade changed in favor of these same groups of goods, particularly machinery and transport equipment. During the post-EEC period, the rate of intra-trade growth was highest for those commodity groups thought to reflect the influence of the EEC to a considerable degree, and least for those not affected by the Common Market. A comparison of the rates of commodity trade growth for the pre-EEC and post-EEC period showed that the effect of the Common Market was most pronounced in the case of machinery and transport equipment.

Along with a change in the commodity composition of intra-EEC trade, the analysis of changes in supply and absorption shares substantially supported the theoretical indications in the case of imports. On the supply side, however, the behavior of export shares was characterized by a deterioration of the dominant supplier's position in favor of the other member countries in the case of virtually every commodity group. There was a generally broader distribution of exports in 1963 than in 1958. Independent changes in supply conditions may have been more powerful than the effects of EEC tariff reductions. Similar conclusions were drawn when the analysis was narrowed to individual commodities.

Whereas both Chapter 5 and Chapter 6, on balance, reached conclusions generally supporting the idea of a pervasive EEC effect on intra-community trade patterns and growth, it was necessary to determine the fundamental reasons underlying these changes. Specifically, was the trade growth and the changes in the direction of intra-EEC trade due to a change in the locus of production within the Common Market, or was it based on changes in demand patterns in response to declining tariff barriers?

This question was the subject of Chapter 7. It was concluded that the proportion of total EEC industrial output contributed by each member country changed substantially during 1958-63. However, there was little obvious evidence of the effect of the EEC, and Germany and Italy gained at the expense of the rest of the EEC nations both during 1958-63 and 1953-58. This was found to hold both for total industrial production as well as that part of industrial output consumed or used within the confines of the Common Market. However, there was little reason for expecting a marked EEC effect on the locus of over-all industrial output, since changes in the locus of production of individual goods would tend to offset each other, thereby leaving the over-all relative output shares more or less unchanged.

The analysis of changes in relative output shares for individual selected commodities, however, showed a similar pattern. There was little evidence of changes in the supply patterns along the lines of the a priori analysis based on the theory of economic integration. It was found that the dominant supplier country in the majority of cases gradually lost its position, resulting in a somewhat more even distribution of production throughout the Common Market. This rejection of the notion that widespread changes in the locus of production of individual commodities would accompany economic integration was supported by an analysis of the relative importance of intra-EEC exports, with respect to total output, for a variety of individual commodities.

When the evidence rejecting the idea of substantial production reallocation is viewed alongside the evidence apparently supporting a substantial EEC effect on trade, it is only possible to conclude that the consumption effect was substantially more important than the production effect as a force affecting internal trade volumes. That is, the high rate of internal trade growth, and the change in direction of EEC trade, which occurred as a result of the formation of the Common Market, reflected primarily a broadening of consumption patterns in each member country, encompassing all of the EEC, with considerable cross-trading of similar or identical commodities. Undoubtedly, the Common Market did result in increased competition among producers in the various member states, but this heightened competition did not result in a reallocation of production to any significant degree. Nonetheless, it was pointed out, increased competition resulting from the removal of internal tariffs could easily have stimulated productive efficiency even in the absence of substantial production shifts.

The purpose of this study has been to present the theoretical prospects for trade and production patterns within an area undergoing economic integration, adapt them to the Common Market institutional framework, and determine whether they are borne out by the facts. Again, it must be said that this study suffers from the same limitations bearing on any study which attempts to isolate the effects of a single variable in a highly complex phenomenon. Nevertheless, it does indicate further, profitable research in this area and reaches at least initial conclusions as to the impact of an economic union on trade among its members.

Note to Chapter 8

1. P.J. Verdoorn, "The Intra-Bloc Trade of the Benelux," in E.A.G. Robinson (ed.), *Economic Consequences of the Size of Nations* (London: Macmillan, 1960).

STATISTICAL APPENDIX

Table 1

Hypothetical Comparison Between Weighted and Unweighted Mean Tariff Levels--Two-Country, Two-Commodity, Limited Case[1]

Country	Tariff on Good X	Annual Value of Imports of X	Col. 2 x Col. 3	Tariff on Good Y	Annual Value of Imports of Y	Col. 5 x Col. 6	Weighted Mean Tariff	Unweighted Mean Tariff
	(1)	(2)	(3)	(4)	(5)	(6)	(7)	(8)
A	20%	10.0	2.0	80%	0.1	0.080	20.4%	50%
B	20%	10.0	2.0	30%	40.0	12.000	28.4%	25%

1 Import values in millions of units of account; tariffs in per cent *ad valorem*.

Table 2

Exports of EEC Countries by Destination*
(in millions of U. S. dollars)

	FRANCE			GERMANY			ITALY		
Year	Total Export	EEC Export	Rest of World Export	Total Export	EEC Export	Rest of World Export	Total Export	EEC Export	Rest of World Export
1953	3,783.6	744.5	3,039.1	4,421.6	1,317.2	3,104.4	1,506.8	310.2	1,196.6
1954	4,188.7	915.1	3,273.6	5,260.6	1,533.2	3,727.4	1,638.3	365.0	1,282.3
1955	4,913.6	1,180.4	3,733.2	6,138.4	1,768.4	4,370.0	1,856.5	454.6	1,401.9
1956	4,541.3	1,148.2	3,393.1	7,360.8	2,169.1	5,191.7	2,156.8	543.1	1,631.7
1957	5,110.4	1,272.6	3,827.8	8,578.4	2,503.4	6,075.0	2,549.7	635.6	1,914.1
1958	5,124.0	1,128.2	3,995.8	8,808.3	2,400.2	6,408.1	2,268.8	600.7	1,668.1
1959	5,616.6	1,524.3	4,092.3	9,816.7	2,724.3	7,092.4	2,784.5	792.1	1,992.4
1960	6,876.5	2,040.1	4,836.4	11,424.1	3,360.1	8,064.0	3,360.4	1,080.0	2,280.4
1961	7,224.5	2,412.4	4,812.1	12,684.6	4,020.5	8,664.1	4,032.7	1,320.4	2,712.3

Table 2, Continued

Year	FRANCE Total Export	FRANCE EEC Export	FRANCE Rest of World Export	GERMANY Total Export	GERMANY EEC Export	GERMANY Rest of World Export	ITALY Total Export	ITALY EEC Export	ITALY Rest of World Export
1962	7,368.1	2,712.1	4,656.0	13,261.1	4,500.8	8,760.3	4,524.1	1,632.1	2,892.0
1963	8,064.6	3,027.2	4,992.4	14,616.2	5,448.1	9,168.1	5,076.9	1,800.6	3,276.3
1964	8,990.4	3,487.2	5,503.2	16,213.3	5,909.8	10,303.5	5,956.3	2,265.9	3,690.4
1965	10,055.4	4,117.1	5,938.3	17,929.7	6,310.4	11,619.3	7,137.4	2,869.9	4,267.5
	NETHERLANDS			BELGIUM-LUXEMBOURG			TOTAL EEC		
1953	2,150.2	765.1	1,385.1	2,259.3	868.0	1,391.3	14,121.5	4,005.0	10,116.5
1954	2,412.0	862.3	1,549.7	2,303.5	991.9	1,311.6	15,803.1	4,658.5	11,134.6
1955	2,687.5	1,028.5	1,659.0	2,779.2	1,241.2	1,538.0	18,375.2	5,673.1	12,702.1
1956	2,862.2	1,156.8	1,705.4	3,162.5	1,416.4	1,746.1	20,083.6	6,433.6	13,650.0
1957	3,097.9	1,287.9	1,810.0	3,186.0	1,468.1	1,699.9	22,522.4	7,167.6	15,344.8
1958	3,116.9	1,332.1	1,784.8	3,048.7	1,368.4	1,680.3	22,366.7	6,829.6	15,537.1

(continued)

Table 2, Continued

	NETHERLANDS			BELGIUM-LUXEMBOURG			TOTAL EEC		
Year	Total Export	EEC Export	Rest of World Export	Total Export	EEC Export	Rest of World Export	Total Export	EEC Export	Rest of World Export
1959	3,712.4	1,596.4	2,116.0	3,300.1	1,524.0	1,776.1	25,230.3	8,161.1	17,069.2
1960	4,032.1	1,848.0	2,184.1	3,744.7	1,884.6	1,860.1	29,437.8	10,212.8	19,225.0
1961	4,308.2	2,040.1	2,268.1	3,912.1	2,088.1	1,824.0	32,161.1	11,881.5	20,280.6
1962	4,585.3	2,256.1	2,328.6	4,345.0	2,460.3	1,884.7	34,083.6	13,562.0	20,521.6
1963	4,968.2	2,652.0	2,316.2	4,860.4	2,952.4	1,908.0	37,586.3	15,925.3	21,661.0
1964	5,908.1	3,233.1	2,575.0	5,579.8	3,493.6	2,086.2	42,548.3	18,390.0	24,158.3
1965	6,392.5	3,560.8	2,831.7	6,386.9	3,956.8	2,430.1	47,901.9	20,815.0	27,086.9

Table 3

Imports of EEC Countries by Origin*
(in millions of U.S. dollars)

	FRANCE			GERMANY			ITALY		
Year	Total Import	EEC Import	Rest of World Import	Total Import	EEC Import	Rest of World Import	Total Import	EEC Import	Rest of World Import
1953	3,938.2	631.4	3,336.8	3,809.5	957.8	2,851.7	2,420.3	532.1	1,888.2
1954	4,215.2	718.3	3,496.9	4,601.0	1,124.1	3,476.9	2,439.1	599.9	1,839.2
1955	4,739.0	945.5	3,793.5	5,821.9	1,502.9	4,319.0	2,711.4	648.0	2,063.4
1956	5,553.0	1,171.2	4,381.8	6,660.6	1,569.7	5,090.9	3,169.1	698.0	2,471.1
1957	6,169.7	1,311.9	4,857.8	7,549.1	1,763.5	5,785.6	3,673.6	785.1	2,888.5
1958	5,607.6	1,226.4	4,381.2	7,412.4	1,897.2	5,515.2	3,170.4	684.0	2,486.4
1959	5,094.9	1,362.0	3,732.0	8,371.2	2,461.2	5.910.0	3,363.6	895.2	2,468.4
1960	6,282.0	1,848.0	4,434.0	10,164.0	3,025.2	7,138.8	4,747.2	1,316.4	3,430.8
1961	6,672.0	2,102.4	4,551.6	10,940.4	3,427.2	7,513.2	5,268.0	1,545.6	3,722.4

(continued)

Table 3, Continued

	FRANCE			GERMANY			ITALY		
Year	Total Import	EEC Import	Rest of World Import	Total Import	EEC Import	Rest of World Import	Total Import	EEC Import	Rest of World Import
1962	7,521.6	2,523.6	4,998.0	12,279.6	3,996.0	8,283.6	6,077.2	1,900.8	4,176.4
1963	8,730.0	3,120.0	5,610.0	13,018.8	4,341.6	8,677.2	7,580.4	2,488.8	5,091.6
1964	10,066.7	3,762.2	6,304.5	14,613.3	5,097.7	9,515.6	7,231.3	2,364.6	4,866.7
1965	10,344.6	4,018.0	6,326.6	17,624.8	6,663.4	10,961.4	7,347.7	2,294.6	5,053.1
	NETHERLANDS			BELGIUM-LUXEMBOURG			ALL-EEC		
1953	2,397.1	881.2	1,515.9	2,422.5	934.2	1,488.3	14,987.6	3,936.7	11,050.9
1954	2,856.5	1,078.9	1,767.6	2,549.9	1,031.6	1,518.3	16,661.7	4,552.8	12,108.9
1955	3,208.1	1,305.2	1,902.9	2,844.0	1,168.0	1,676.0	19,324.4	5,569.6	13,754.8
1956	3,712.5	1,535.4	2,177.1	3,272.5	1,350.9	1,921.6	22,367.7	6,325.2	16,042.5
1957	4,105.1	1,688.3	2,416.8	3,432.4	1,493.9	1,938.5	24,929.9	7,042.7	17,887.2
1958	3,625.6	1,518.0	2,107.6	3,135.6	1,461.6	1,674.0	22,951.6	6,787.2	16,164.4

Table 3, Continued

	NETHERLANDS			BELGIUM-LUXEMBOURG			ALL-EEC		
Year	Total Import	EEC Import	Rest of World Import	Total Import	EEC Import	Rest of World Import	Total Import	EEC Import	Rest of World Import
1959	3,938.4	1,749.6	2,560.8	3,444.0	1,621.2	1,822.8	24,211.2	8,089.2	16,122.0
1960	4,531.2	2,076.0	2,467.2	3,889.2	1,867.2	2,022.0	29,613.6	10,132.0	19,480.8
1961	5,112.0	2,514.0	2,598.0	4,164.0	2,107.2	2,056.8	32,156.4	11,696.4	20,460.0
1962	5,347.2	2,683.2	2,664.0	4,471.2	2,292.0	2,169.2	32,696.8	13,395.6	19,301.2
1963	5,967.6	3,081.6	2,886.0	5,112.0	2,688.0	2,424.0	40,408.8	15,720.0	24,688.8
1964	7,055.0	3,670.8	3,384.2	5,901.2	3,145.9	2,755.3	44,867.2	18,041.0	26,826.2
1965	7,462.5	3,986.3	3,476.2	6,359.7	3,463.2	2,896.5	49,139.3	20,425.5	28,713.8

*Sources: United Nations, Statistical Office, Statistical Papers, Series T, The Direction of International Trade (New York), 1956-58 and 1953-56; Organization for Economic Cooperation and Development, Foreign Trade Statistics (Paris), 1960, 1965, 1966; Organization for Economic Cooperation and Development, General Statistics (Paris), 1960, 1965, 1966; Office Statistique des Communautés Européennes, Tableaux Analytiques, "Import" (Luxembourg), 1964, 1965, 1966.

Table 4

Movements in Export Prices for EEC Countries and Regional Import Deflator [2] (1958 = 100)

Year	France		Germany		Italy		Netherlands		Belgium-Luxembourg	
	EPI	RMD	EPI	RMD	EPI	RMD	EPI	RMD	EPI	RMD
1953	86	102	98	99	110	96	99	97	101	98
1954	81	99	95	95	107	92	97	95	95	95
1955	82	99	96	96	104	94	99	95	98	95
1956	85	101	98	96	101	97	101	97	104	96
1957	90	104	101	102	105	101	104	101	107	100
1958	100	100	100	100	100	100	100	100	100	100
1959	109	97	98	99	92	101	100	100	96	99
1960	114	98	101	101	96	102	99	103	98	101
1961	113	97	102	99	92	101	98	100	97	100
1962	113	97	102	98	93	100	97	100	96	100
1963	115	98	101	101	95	103	99	103	96	103
1964	119	101	104	105	96	106	102	105	98	106
1965	121	104	107	106	97	108	104	107	98	108

EPI = export price index.

RMD = regional import deflator; computed as the weighted arithmetic mean of the export price indexes of the four remaining EEC countries, with the weights being the percentage of total national intra-EEC imports supplied by each country. Hence the regional import deflator is simply an import price index applying exclusively to imports from the EEC.

[2] Data: EPI: IMF, International Financial Statistics, 1962, 1965; RMD: Each country's EPI weighted by import shares taken from OEEC/OECD, Foreign Trade Statistics, various issues, 1953-65 inclusive.

Table 5

Movements in Wholesale Prices and GNP
(in current prices for EEC countries, 1953-65, local currencies)[3]

Year	France			Germany			Italy		
	PI	GNP	Change	WPI	GNP	Change	WPI	GNP	Change
1953	83	150.4		97	145.5		99	11,831	
			(5.8)			(7.5)			(6.6)
1954	81	159.2		96	156.4		98	12,616	
			(7.0)			(14.0)			(8.7)
1955	81	170.5		97	178.3		99	13,807	
			(10.4)			(10.2)			(7.9)
1956	85	188.3		99	196.4		101	14,885	
			(10.8)			(8.8)			(7.4)
1957	90	210.6		100	213.6		102	15,992	
			(16.2)			(8.8)			(7.0)
1958	100	244.7		100	231.5		100	17,114	
			(6.2)			(7.1)			(6.2)
1959	105	260.0		99	247.9		97	18,290	
			(13.9)			(19.7)			(8.9)
1960	107	296.2		100	296.8		98	19,937	
			(7.9)			(9.9)			(10.4)
1961	110	319.7		102	326.2		98	22,022	
			(10.6)			(8.7			(12.5)
1962	113	353.6		103	354.5		101	24,789	
			(10.7)			(6.2)			(13.3)

(continued)

Table 5, Continued

Year	France			Germany			Italy		
	PI	GNP	Change	WPI	GNP	Change	WPI	GNP	Change
1963	116	391.8		103	376.5		106	28,186	
			(10.2)			(9.8)			(9.8)
1964	119	431.9		108	413.4		110	30,950	
			(5.6)			(8.4)			(6.6)
1965	121	456.0		115	448.0		112	33,000	

Year	Netherlands			BLEU		
	WPI	GNP	Change	PI	GNP	Change
1953	95	24.3		98	449	
			(11.5)			(7.4)
1954	96	27.1		97	472	
			(11.7)			(5.3)
1955	97	30.3		99	497	
			(7.2)			(8.0)
1956	99	32.5		102	536	
			(8.6)			(4.6)
1957	102	35.3		104	561	
			(1.7)			(1.2)
1958	100	35.9		100	568	
			(6.9)			(3.7)
1959	101	38.4		100	589	
			(11.2)			(6.4)
1960	99	43.7		101	627	
			(6.1)			(0.5)

Table 5, Continued

Year	Netherlands			BLEU		
	WPI	GNP	Change	PI	GNP	Change
1961	98	45.3		101	630	
			(6.2)			(5.7)
1962	99	48.1		101	666	
			(8.5)			(7.4)
1963	101	52.2		103	716	
			(16.5)			(7.3)
1964	107	60.8		109	768	
			(7.6)			(5.7)
1965	111	65.4		110	812	

PI - Prices of Home and Import Goods, 1958 = 100;

WPI - Wholesale Price Index, 1958 = 100;

GNP - Gross National Product in Current Prices, local currencies (i.e., France = NF, Germany = DM, Italy = Lire, Netherlands = Hfl., BLEU = Bfr.);

Change - Percentage rates of growth in money GNP.

---

[3]Data: IMF, International Financial Statistics (Washington, D.C.: IMF, 1959, 1966. All data for 1965 are preliminary.

Table 6

GNP Implicit Price Deflators, EEC Countries, 1953-63[4]
(1953 = 100)

Year	France	Germany	Italy	Netherlands	Belgium-Luxembourg*
1953	100	100	100	100	100
1954	101	100	101	104	101
1955	102	102	104	108	103
1956	108	105	108	112	109
1957	114	109	109	119	113
1958	127	113	112	120	113
1959	134	115	111	122	112
1960	139	118	113	124	114
1961	144	123	115	126	117
1962	150	125	123	131	119
1963	154	127	129	135	122
1964	158	129	134	138	125
1965	163	132	139	143	128

* Weighted average of the figures for Belgium-Luxembourg, composed of the implicit GNP deflator for each country weighted by the proportion of total GNP contributed by that country to the Belgium- Luxembourg Economic Union.

---

[4] Sources: 1953-57 from OECD, General Statistics, November, 1962, p. vii; 1962 and 1963 calculated from European Communities Statistical Office, Allgemeines Statistisches Bulletin, 1963, No. 7-8, pp. 13-17, and 1964, No. 7-8, pp. 12-16; 1965, ibid. 1965 data are estimates.

Table 7

GNP of Common Market Countries at Market Prices, 1953-57 and 1963-65 (in billions of U.S. dollars, translated at prevailing exchange rates)[5]

Year	Prices	France	Germany	Italy	Nether-lands	Belg.-Lux.
1953	current	42.66	34.34	18.71	6.40	8.82
	1953	42.66	34.34	18.71	6.40	8.82
1954	current	45.12	37.24	19.96	7.12	9.21
	1953	44.67	37.24	19.76	6.85	9.12
1955	current	48.63	42.30	21.83	7.92	9.68
	1953	47.68	41.47	20.99	7.33	9.40
1956	current	53.13	46.06	23.41	8.55	10.41
	1953	49.19	43.87	21.68	7.63	9.55
1957	current	55.02	50.83	25.10	9.34	11.21
	1953	49.26	46.63	23.03	7.85	9.92
1963	current	79.89	94.72	45.25	14.49	13.94
	1953	52.56	74.58	35.08	10.73	11.43
1964	current	88.1	103.4	49.6	16.89	15.2
	1953	55.8	80.2	37.0	12.24	12.2
1965	current	93.1	112.0	52.8	18.17	16.9
	1953	57.1	84.8	38.0	12.70	13.2

[5] Data: Current GNP and exchange rate figures from International Financial Statistics (Washington, D.C.: IMF), various issues, 1953-65 inclusive. GNP implicit price deflators from Appendix Table 6.

Table 8

Intra-EEC Imports in Current and 1958 Prices, 1953-57 and 1963 [6] (in billions of U.S. dollars)

Year	Prices	France	Germany	Italy	Nether-lands	Belg.-Lux.
1953	current	0.6314	0.9578	0.5321	0.8812	0.9342
	1958	0.6190	0.9675	0.5543	0.9085	0.9533
1954	current	0.7183	1.1241	0.5999	1.0789	1.0316
	1958	0.7256	1.1833	0.6521	1.1366	1.0859
1955	current	0.9455	1.5029	0.6480	1.3052	1.1680
	1958	0.9551	1.5655	0.6894	1.3739	1.1229
1956	current	1.1712	1.5697	0.6980	1.5354	1.3509
	1958	1.1596	1.6351	0.7196	1.6829	1.4072
1957	current	1.3119	1.7635	0.7861	1.6883	1.4939
	1958	1.2614	1.7289	0.7773	1.6716	1.4939
1963	current	3.1200	4.3416	2.4888	3.0816	2.6880
	1958	3.1837	4.2986	2.4163	2.9918	2.6097
1964	current	3.7622	5.0977	2.3646	3.6708	3.1459
	1958	3.7250	4.8550	2.2308	3.4960	2.9678
1965	current	4.0180	6.6634	2.2946	3.9863	3.4632
	1958	3.7264	6.3035	2.0406	3.5577	3.0981

[6] Data: Appendix Tables 3 and 4.

Table 9

Change in the Direction of EEC Trade, 1953-63 [7]
(per cent)

a) Percentage of total exports destined for the EEC:

Year	France	Germany	Italy	Nether-lands	Belg.-Lux.	EEC
1953	19.7	29.8	20.6	35.6	38.4	28.4
1954	21.8	29.1	22.3	35.7	43.1	29.5
1955	24.0	28.8	24.5	38.3	44.7	30.9
1956	25.3	29.5	25.2	40.4	44.8	32.0
1957	24.9	29.2	24.9	41.6	46.1	31.8
1958	22.0	27.2	26.5	42.7	41.6	30.5
1959	27.1	27.8	28.4	43.0	46.2	32.3
1960	29.7	29.4	32.1	45.8	50.3	34.7
1961	33.4	31.7	32.7	47.4	53.4	36.9
1962	36.8	33.9	36.1	49.2	56.6	39.8
1963	37.5	37.8	35.5	53.4	60.7	42.4
1964	38.8	36.5	38.0	54.7	62.6	43.2
1965	40.9	35.2	40.2	55.7	62.0	43.5

b) Percentage of total imports originating in EEC:

Year	France	Germany	Italy	Nether-lands	Belg.-Lux.	EEC
1953	16.3	25.1	22.0	36.8	38.6	26.3
1954	17.0	24.4	24.5	37.8	40.5	27.3
1955	19.9	25.8	24.0	40.7	41.1	28.8
1956	21.1	23.6	22.0	41.4	41.3	28.3
1957	21.3	23.4	21.4	41.1	43.5	28.3
1958	21.9	25.6	21.6	41.9	46.6	29.6
1959	26.7	29.4	26.6	44.5	47.1	33.4
1960	29.4	29.8	27.7	45.8	48.0	34.2
1961	31.5	31.3	29.3	49.2	50.6	36.4
1962	33.6	32.5	31.3	50.2	51.3	37.5
1963	35.7	33.3	32.8	51.6	52.6	38.9
1964	37.4	34.9	32.7	52.0	53.3	40.2
1965	38.8	37.8	31.2	53.4	54.5	41.6

[7] Based on data in current prices, Appendix Tables 2 and 3.

Table 10

Comparative Trade Growth, 1953-63 (millions of U.S. dollars or index 1953=100)[8]

Year	Intra-EEC	Intra-EFTA	Intra-OECD* (Excluding EEC)	Intra-European OECD (Excluding EEC)	Intra-North America	World (Index)
1953	334	190	1,302	847	455	100
1954	388	201	1,307	879	428	106
1955	471	213	1,499	1,016	483	118
1956	536	227	1,661	1,091	570	127
1957	597	243	2,644	1,188	576	135
1958	566	233	2,480	1,143	530	133
1959	674	299	2,715	1,225	584	144
1960	845	288	3,049	1,425	565	161
1961	975	315	3,190	1,582	563	169
1962	1,116	335	3,388	1,710	605	181
1963	1,311	356	3,290	1,690	640	193

* Non-EEC OECD comprises Canada, United States, Austria, Denmark, Greece, Ireland, Norway, Portugal, Sweden, United Kingdom, and Yugoslavia.

[8] Data: OECD, General Statistics (Paris, 1963); U.N., Direction of International Trade (New York), 1964, 1958. All data in current prices.

Table 11

Projected Average Propensities to Import[9] from the EEC, 1965 (per cent)

	France	Germany	Italy	Nether- lands	Belg. - Lux.
Assumption I	2.3	3.7	3.3	20.2	13.9
Assumption II	4.3	3.7	3.3	27.6	21.4

[9] Data: See note to Table 15.

Table 12

Calculated and Actual 1965 Intra-EEC Imports
(millions of U.S. dollars at 1958 prices)[10]

Country	(1) 1965 Calculated Imports (Assumption I)	(2) 1965 Calculated Imports (Assumption II)	(3) 1965 Actual Imports	(4) % of * Actual Attributed to EEC (Assumption I)	(5) % of ** Actual Attributed to EEC (Assumption II)
France	1,311.3	2,455.3	4,018.0	67.4	38.9
Germany	3,137.6	3,137.6	6,663.4	52.9	52.9
Italy	1,254.0	1,254.0	2,294.6	45.3	45.3
Netherlands	2,565.4	3,505.2	3,986.3	35.6	12.1
Belg.-Lux.	1,834.8	2,824.8	3,463.2	47.0	18.4
Total EEC	10,103.1	13,176.9	20,425.5	50.5	35.5

* Column 3 less column 1 divided by column 3, times one hundred.
** Column 3 less column 2 divided by column 3, times one hundred.

[10] Data: See note to Table 16.

Table 13

Commodity Exports of EEC Countries to the Common Market, 1953 and 1958-63 (millions of U.S. dollars)[11]

SITC Class*	Year	Belg.-Lux.	France	Germany	Italy	Nether-lands
	1953	43.1	70.2	21.7	134.6	299.7
	1958	87.6	124.4	70.8	213.4	410.3
	1959	98.9	176.7	76.9	257.4	515.8
0 + 1	1960	110.0	266.2	100.8	272.1	564.8
	1961	131.1	353.5	105.3	315.3	549.4
	1962	177.1	355.0	100.9	-	-
	1963	229.5	362.5	111.0	325.7	719.7
	1953	105.6	184.5	59.9	31.8	77.3
	1958	106.1	214.7	110.2	42.7	114.0
	1959	131.6	316.9	133.0	50.6	130.7
2	1960	154.5	396.6	172.8	59.8	167.2
	1961	163.5	388.9	190.3	69.2	186.0
	1962	180.2	-	198.9	-	-
	1963	222.3	395.6	206.1	70.4	226.8
	1953	94.8	92.1	311.7	3.1	56.4
	1958	103.2	57.8	397.1	16.3	142.5
	1959	91.8	61.8	415.1	27.5	151.1
3	1960	96.3	41.7	479.4	39.7	177.7
	1961	87.2	40.6	471.1	29.2	190.9
	1962	90.2	-	477.9	-	-
	1963	127.5	28.8	434.4	55.2	261.6
	1953	8.0	3.8	3.3	0.4	25.6
	1958	5.5	3.4	6.6	0.9	17.1
	1959	6.2	4.4	8.0	1.1	19.3
4	1960	8.6	4.9	10.6	1.6	27.5
	1961	9.7	6.5	8.1	1.9	21.3
	1962	10.6	-	8.4	-	-
	1963	7.7	6.8	12.4	2.1	21.7

(continued)

Table 13, Continued

SITC Class*	Year	Belg.-Lux.	France	Germany	Italy	Netherlands
	1953	42.3	56.3	100.8	11.3	33.0
	1958	72.4	97.7	208.2	29.1	87.2
	1959	81.8	117.2	252.4	36.0	97.0
5	1960	106.2	150.3	317.9	58.7	107.7
	1961	108.4	178.5	350.4	71.3	131.1
	1962	123.6	-	393.5	-	-
	1963	139.4	214.7	472.2	95.2	173.7
	1953	74.8	84.3	432.2	41.2	75.5
	1958	206.2	175.1	808.1	150.5	173.9
	1959	217.4	282.4	877.5	187.9	205.6
7	1960	275.5	380.0	1,072.0	255.0	255.4
	1961	360.1	523.1	1,418.2	345.2	316.8
	1962	428.0	-	1,842.8	-	-
	1963	578.2	543.2	2,292.4	545.8	501.5
	1953	464.1	271.8	327.1	74.4	183.8
	1958	757.6	450.3	559.7	208.6	360.7
	1959	857.6	640.2	791.1	282.0	425.7
6 + 8	1960	1,092.4	772.1	1,133.9	357.7	505.5
	1961	1,180.4	933.1	1,303.8	455.4	546.0
	1962	1,367.5	-	1,461.6	-	-
	1963	1,583.0	972.4	1,748.4	685.9	721.0

* Standard International Trade Classification:

0 + 1 Food, beverages, and tobacco.
2 Crude materials, inedible, except fuels.
3 Mineral fuels, lubricants, and related materials.
4 Animal and vegetable oils and fats.
5 Chemicals.
7 Machinery and transport equipment.
6 + 8 Other manufactured goods.

- not calculated.

[11]United Nations, Secretariat, Statistical Office, Statistical Papers, Series D, various volumes, 1953, 1954, and 1958-65 (data).

Table 14

Commodity Imports of EEC Countries from the Common Market, 1953 and 1958-63 (millions of U. S. dollars)[12]

SITC Class	Year	Belg.-Lux.	France	Germany	Netherlands	Italy
	1953	139.4	57.1	307.0	29.2	36.6
	1958	155.2	92.0	503.9	79.7	77.7
	1959	175.8	142.1	631.0	87.2	89.6
0 + 1	1960	184.5	172.9	432.4	129.1	102.6
	1961	196.8	145.5	842.2	126.3	143.8
	1962	204.1	200.2	964.6	138.9	133.6
	1963	238.0	231.3	964.2	149.5	240.4
	1953	14.2	46.4	126.3	69.8	77.0
	1958	65.1	76.8	170.3	104.9	78.3
	1959	182.5	76.5	230.4	167.5	96.2
2	1960	210.3	97.8	302.4	221.5	153.4
	1961	228.5	117.0	311.8	224.1	116.5
	1962	249.8	120.3	336.3	246.7	126.7
	1963	261.0	122.4	338.3	259.5	140.0
	1953	98.7	202.9	80.5	80.7	95.3
	1958	194.0	281.0	120.1	106.7	42.1
	1959	193.5	366.0	117.1	111.9	39.7
3	1960	201.4	322.4	112.4	127.5	71.1
	1961	212.1	301.6	99.1	139.7	66.6
	1962	227.2	285.1	146.7	146.1	64.0
	1963	226.1	282.1	192.8	159.6	50.4
	1953	2.5	0.5	10.2	1.8	5.7
	1958	7.2	2.3	12.7	5.1	6.2
	1959	8.1	2.2	14.2	6.1	8.4
4	1960	8.1	6.2	22.8	4.6	11.2
	1961	9.1	9.5	18.0	5.1	5.8
	1962	10.4	15.8	18.5	5.6	6.5
	1963	11.2	17.2	17.7	8.8	9.0

(continued)

Table 14, Continued

SITC Class	Year	Belg.-Lux.	France	Germany	Netherlands	Italy
	1953	73.6	35.8	35.3	62.1	36.7
	1958	131.5	79.3	76.7	116.0	82.1
	1959	144.8	94.6	104.6	136.3	104.1
5	1960	157.0	129.2	144.2	167.7	142.7
	1961	180.7	163.7	156.1	180.5	158.5
	1962	193.4	205.7	179.5	184.4	185.5
	1963	222.1	237.8	211.7	213.2	220.4
	1953	203.0	144.5	240.5	201.7	118.3
	1958	383.7	305.8	208.8	454.2	162.4
	1959	422.7	326.4	313.3	506.8	201.6
7	1960	526.0	408.1	386.4	603.6	313.8
	1961	630.2	564.8	509.1	815.2	444.1
	1962	725.4	739.6	615.5	944.1	615.9
	1963	851.4	821.4	636.5	1,105.3	884.4
	1953	275.3	122.1	331.2	435.4	157.2
	1958	425.7	389.2	776.2	658.2	207.4
	1959	489.5	432.7	1,017.6	782.9	273.9
6 + 8	1960	596.2	710.9	1,208.8	931.7	411.0
	1961	671.5	801.2	1,366.4	1,073.2	506.4
	1962	713.6	962.2	1,556.8	1,092.7	626.0
	1963	857.7	1,021.4	1,698.8	1,226.6	794.0

[12] Data: See Table 13, note.

Table 15

EEC Commodity Price Indexes, 1953, 1958, and 1963[13]

Country	Index	1953	1958	1963
France	Farm Products	77	100	116
	Raw Materials	92	100	118
	Finished Goods	88	100	119
	Export Prices	86	100	119
Germany	Farm Products	85	100	107
	Raw Materials	95	100	101
	Finished Goods	94	100	107
	Export Prices	98	100	101
Italy	Farm Products	90	100	109
	Raw Materials	98	100	99
	Finished Goods	98	100	107
	Export Prices	110	100	96
Netherlands	Farm Products	102	100	105
	Raw Materials	91	100	94
	Finished Goods	95	100	102
	Export Prices	99	100	99
Belgium-Luxembourg	Farm Products	104	100	111
	Raw Materials	98	100	102
	Finished Goods	98	100	105
	Export Prices	101	100	96

[13] Data: United Nations, Monthly Bulletin of Statistics, various issues, 1960-65; IMF, International Financial Statistics, various issues, 1960-65.

Table 16

Trade of Common Market Countries in Selected Commodities, 1954, 1958, and 1963 (metric tons)[14]

SITC Commodity Code*	1954 Total Exports	1954 Total Imports	1954 Intra-Trade	1958 Total Exports	1958 Total Imports	1958 Intra-Trade
046	445, 793	192, 452	3, 460	1, 062, 199	345, 375	160, 587
122	4, 009	2, 925	1, 200	7, 631	5, 930	3, 319
112	817, 976	1, 920, 485	213, 478	821, 622	2, 520, 506	285, 446
266	82, 383	20, 095	6, 535	144, 180	29, 206	13, 059
512	478, 617	347, 855	157, 470	809, 689	781, 205	293, 273
665	163, 425	100, 686	69, 821	220, 091	137, 260	92, 599
715	171, 976	110, 252	45, 018	257, 347	90, 583	53, 445
721	390, 930	124, 322	82, 014	534, 458	177, 163	121, 951
541	29, 000	12, 643	2, 953	42, 058	14, 442	6, 141
732	607, 095	236, 007	134, 202	1, 352, 974	351, 946	264, 524
851	17, 925	6, 151	3, 477	30, 019	11, 064	6, 474
821	46, 479	15, 895	12, 236	68, 299	36, 100	24, 159

14 Data: See following page.

*See code key on following page.

Table 16, Continued

SITC Commodity Code*	1963 Total Exports	1963 Total Imports	1963 Intra-Trade
046	1,083,982	84,638	15,442
122	18,165	12,680	9,456
112	1,113,233	2,535,439	573,875
266	232,750	80,978	47,508
512	2,283,496	2,195,228	831,051
665	388,429	243,425	182,300
715	382,095	254,618	147,541
721	863,842	284,601	197,335
541	198,515	56,822	17,609
732	2,433,870	1,203,264	936,890
851	59,390	37,911	23,382
821	148,639	131,397	92,464

*SITC Commodity Code:

046 Wheat flours and meal
122 Manufactured tobacco
112 Alcoholic beverages
266 Synthetic fibers
512 Organic chemicals
665 Glassware
715 Metalworking machinery
721 Electric power machinery, switchgear, etc.
541 Drugs
732 Road motor vehicles
851 Footwear
821 Furniture

Data: United Nations, Secretariat, Statistical Office, Statistical Papers, Series D (New York: United Nations), 1953, 1958, 1963; Commerce Extérieur, Série 3 (Paris: OEEC), 1953, 1958; Organization for Economic Cooperation and Development, Foreign Trade Statistics, Series C (Paris: OECD), 1963; European Communities, Statistical Office, Analytische Uebersichten: Ausfuhr and Analytische Uebersichten: Einfuhr (Luxembourg: European Communities, 1963).

Table 17

Change in the Pattern of Industrial Production Among EEC Countries, 1953, 1958, and 1963[15] (millions of 1958 U.S. dollars)*

Year	Country	(1) Total Industrial Production	(2) Of Which Total Exports	(3) Non-EEC Exports	(4) (Col. 1-Col. 2) Consumed Domestically	(5) (Col. 2-Col. 3) Consumed in Rest of EEC	(6) (Col. 4+Col. 5) Output Consumed in EEC	
1953	Belg.-Lux.	2,470	1,194	356	1,276	838	2,114	
	France	17,457	4,250	3,424	13,207	816	14,023	
	Germany	14,571	4,476	3,143	10,095	1,333	11,428	
	Italy	5,155	1,160	956	3,995	204	4,199	
	Netherl.	1,989	762	139	1,227	623	1,850	
								33,614
1958	Belg.-Lux.	2,906	1,920	545	986	1,325	2,311	
	France	18,304	4,941	3,874	13,363	1,067	14,430	
	Germany	22,188	8,706	6,339	13,482	2,367	15,849	
	Italy	7,375	1,979	1,472	5,396	507	5,903	
	Netherl.	2,535	1,542	410	993	1,132	2,125	
								40,618
1963	Belg.-Lux.	3,807	2,759	685	1,048	2,074	3,122	
	France	23,807	6,648	4,136	17,159	2,512	19,671	
	Germany	31,723	14,314	8,971	17,408	5,343	22,751	
	Italy	12,496	4,824	3,126	7,672	1,698	9,370	
	Netherl.	3,695	2,229	449	1,466	1,780	3,246	
								58,160

Table 17, Continued

* All industrial production data at 1958 factor cost; all exports in 1958 prices. Industrial production data translated into U.S. dollars at exchange rate prevailing at end of year in question.

---

[15]Data: Industrial production - United Nations, *Yearbook of National Accounts Statistics* (New York: United Nations), 1963; and IMF, *International Financial Statistics* (Washington, D.C.: IMF), 1965, 1962/1963.

Export price indexes and exchange rates - IMF, *op. cit.*, *supra.*

Export data: U.N., *Commodity Trade Statistics* (New York: United Nations), 1953, 1958, 1963.

Table 18

Production and Exports of Selected Commodities in EEC, 1953, 1958, and 1963 [16]
(in metric tons)

Canned Fish		Output	(less) World Exports	(equals) Domestic Use	(plus) EEC Exports	(equals) EEC	Use %
1953	Belg.-Lux.	700	404	296	88	384	0.2
	France	69,300	3,362	65,938	241	66,179	39.3
	Germany	90,600	4,034	86,466	839	87,305	51.8
	Italy	2,100	515	1,485	36	1,521	0.9
	Netherlands	16,300	8,605	7,595	5,590	13,185	7.8
1958	Belg.-Lux.	3,500	503	2,997	114	3,111	1.8
	France	55,700	4,916	50,684	75	50,759	29.8
	Germany	93,900	6,553	87,447	1,617	89,064	52.4
	Italy	20,000	813	19,087	153	19,240	11.3
	Netherlands	11,400	6,758	4,542	3,334	7,876	4.6
1963	Belg.-Lux.	2,900	395	2,505	125	2,630	1.6
	France	74,800	2,769	72,031	412	72,443	43.1
	Germany	41,300	5,495	35,705	1,446	37,151	22.0
	Italy	45,000	835	44,165	245	44,410	26.4
	Netherlands	15,300	11,063	4,237	7,254	11,491	6.8

(See note at end of this table.)

Table 18, Continued

		Output	(less) World Exports	(equals) Domestic Use	(plus) EEC Exports	(equals) EEC	Use
Cheese							%
1953	Belg.-Lux.	8,300	362	7,938	73	8,011	0.9
	France	296,000	16,697	279,203	1,165	280,368	32.6
	Germany	163,500	3,827	159,573	3,371	162,944	18.9
	Italy	291,900	14,621	277,279	2,321	279,600	32.5
	Netherlands	159,200	86,045	73,055	55,898	129,053	15.0
1958	Belg.-Lux.	16,000	850	15,150	594	15,744	1.4
	France	427,000	27,637	399,263	2,894	402,257	35.1
	Germany	268,000	7,845	260,155	6,856	267,011	23.3
	Italy	319,300	22,923	296,377	3,773	300,150	26.2
	Netherlands	187,300	97,555	89,645	72,307	162,052	14.1
1963	Belg.-Lux.	31,000	4,563	26,437	4,432	30,869	2.4
	France	432,000	45,779	386,221	28,226	414,447	32.1
	Germany	314,000	18,903	295,098	16,192	311,290	24.1
	Italy	357,000	25,651	331,249	4,561	335,910	26.0
	Netherlands	238,000	117,517	120,383	79,909	198,392	15.4

(continued)

Table 18, Continued

		Output	(less) World Exports	(equals) Domestic Use	(plus) EEC Exports	(equals) EEC	Use
Margarine							%
1953	Belg. -Lux	75,200	14,622	60,478	6,739	63,317	7.8
	France	76,000	16,697	59,303	1,165	60,468	7.0
	Germany	566,000	3,827	562,173	3,371	565,544	65.0
	Italy	neg.	neg.	neg.	neg.	neg.	0
	Netherlands	202,000	86,045	115,955	55,898	171,853	19.9
1958	Belg. -Lux.	101,200	11,465	89,735	583	90,318	10.0
	France	99,000	36,040	62,960	8,556	71,516	7.9
	Germany	603,000	1,362	601,538	870	602,508	66.4
	Italy	neg.	neg.	neg.	neg.	neg.	0
	Netherlands	225,600	94,105	131,495	10,887	142,382	15.7
1963	Belg. -Lux.	119,300	1,492	117,808	1,152	118,960	12.2
	France	123,400	3,767	119,533	208	119,841	12.3
	Germany	532,400	3,150	529,250	1,048	530,298	54.6
	Italy	neg.	neg.	neg.	neg.	neg.	0
	Netherlands	243,600	43,659	199,941	2,844	202,785	20.9

Table 18, Continued

Cement		Output	(less) World Exports	(equals) Domestic Use	(plus) EEC Exports	(equals) EEC	Use %
1953	Belg. -Lux.	4,626,000	2,255,000	2,371,000	220,837	2,591,837	7.9
	France	9,227,000	1,098,000	8,129,000	104,692	8,233,692	25.0
	Germany	15,068,000	2,216,000	12,652,000	739,831	13,591,831	41.2
	Italy	7,832,000	46,420	7,785,580	2,424	7,788,004	23.6
	Netherlands	861,000	156,111	704,489	75,701	780,190	2.3
1958	Belg. -Lux.	4,057,000	1,639,000	2,418,000	1,072,220	2,525,220	5.1
	France	13,629,000	785,609	12,843,291	76,375	12,766,916	26.2
	Germany	19,737,000	1,409,000	18,328,000	965,030	19,293,030	39.6
	Italy	12,838,000	117,470	12,720,530	9,490	12,730,020	26.2
	Netherlands	1,366,000	155,949	1,210,851	132,710	1,343,661	2.8
1963	Belg. -Lux.	4,716,000	1,196,225	3,519,775	834,200	4,353,975	5.8
	France	18,060,000	1,081,338	16,978,662	339,929	17,318,591	23.2
	Germany	29,220,000	783,604	28,436,296	600,698	29,037,094	39.0
	Italy	22,032,000	313,492	21,718,508	4,217	21,722,725	29.2
	Netherlands	2,076,000	7,893	2,068,107	4,524	2,072,631	2.8

(continued)

Table 18, Continued

Zinc		Output	(less) World Exports	(equals) Domestic Use	(plus) EEC Exports	(equals) EEC	Use %
1953	Belg.-Lux.	193,400	139,111	54,289	49,876	104,165	30.7
	France	93,500	2,722	90,778	0	90,778	26.8
	Germany	166,200	45,825	120,375	10,876	131,251	38.7
	Italy	56,900	26,229	30,671	1,694	32,635	9.6
	Netherlands	25,200	20,568	4,632	5,640	10,272	3.0
1958	Belg.-Lux.	214,800	160,001	54,799	74,344	129,143	23.7
	France	178,800	1,992	176,808	97	176,905	32.5
	Germany	191,700	37,200	154,500	10,293	164,793	30.2
	Italy	71,400	14,907	56,493	3,617	60,110	11.0
	Netherlands	26,600	16,220	10,380	3,551	13,931	2.6
1963	Belg.-Lux.	202,400	138,440	63,960	79,660	143,620	22.9
	France	205,900	17,843	188,057	13,329	201,386	32.1
	Germany	194,500	35,527	158,973	8,354	167,372	26.7
	Italy	82,200	606	81,594	22	81,616	13.0
	Netherlands	39,400	24,775	14,625	18,429	33,054	5.3

Table 18, Continued

[16] Data:

a) OEEC/OECD, _General Statistics_ (Paris: OEEC/OECD), various issues, 1953-65 inclusive.
b) United Nations, _Statistical Yearbook_ (New York: U. N.), various issues, 1953-65 inclusive.
c) European Communities, Statistical Office, _Industriestatistik_ (Luxembourg: European Communities), various issues, 1953-65 inclusive.
d) European Communities, Statistical Office, _Aussenhandel: Ausfuhr_ and _Aussenhandel: Einfuhr_ (Luxembourg: European Communities), various issues, 1953-65 inclusive.
e) OEEC, _Foreign Trade Statistics_, Series C (Paris: OEEC), January-December, 1953 and 1958.
f) OECD, _Foreign Trade Statistics_, Series III (Paris: OECD), January-December, 1963.
g) United Nations, Secretariat, Statistical Office, _Statistical Papers_, Series D, _Commodity Trade Statistics_ (New York: United Nations), January-December, 1953, 1958, and 1963.

Table 19

Production and Exports of Selected Commodities in EEC, 1958 and 1963 [17]
(in metric tons and units, as stated)

1958: Wool Fabrics (t)	(1) Total Output	(2) Total Exports	(3) Non-EEC Exports	(4) ((1)-(2)) Consumed Domestically	(5) ((2)-(3)) Consumed in Rest of EEC	((4)+(5)) Output Consumed in EEC
Benelux	38,280	12,693	5,016	25,487	7,677	33,164
France	76,680	4,362	2,794	72,318	1,468	73,786
Germany	63,840	2,749	1,672	61,091	1,077	62,168
Italy	78,000	33,874	19,843	44,026	14,031	58,057
						227,175
Cotton Fabrics (t)						
Benelux	229,300	45,855	31,901	183,445	13,954	197,399
France	234,000	22,674	20,890	211,226	1,784	213,010
Germany	273,600	20,566	17,549	253,034	3,017	256,051
Italy	114,000	10,989	9,610	103,011	1,379	104,390
						770,850

Table 19, Continued

1958: Rayon/Acetate Yarn(t)	(1) Total Output	(2) Total Exports	(3) Non-EEC Exports	(4) ((1)-(2)) Consumed Domestically	(5) ((2)-(3)) Consumed in Rest of EEC	((4)+(5)) Output Consumed in EEC
Benelux	41,760	28,096	17,625	13,664	10,471	24,135
France	56,280	15,319	14,823	40,961	496	41,457
Germany	64,920	18,776	16,917	46,044	1,859	47,903
Italy	61,440	24,370	22,295	37,070	2,075	39,145
						152,640
Agricultural Tractors (#)						
Benelux	2,300	398	77	1,902	321	2,223
France	119,040	72,124	27,824	46,916	44,300	91,216
Germany	171,480	53,021	35,167	118,459	17,854	136,313
Italy	25,560	3	1	25,557	2	25,559
						255,311
Automobiles (#)						
Benelux	139,200	58,211	8,845	80,989	49,366	130,355
France	924,000	325,100	275,778	598,900	49,222	648,122
Germany	1,180,800	566,931	489,189	613,869	77,742	691,611
Italy	379,200	8,817	762	370,383	8,055	378,438
						1,848,526

(continued)

Table 19, Continued

1958:	(1)	(2)	(3)	(4)	(5)	
			Non-	((1)-(2))	((2)-(3))	((4)+(5))
Commercial Vehicles (#)	Total Output	Total Exports	EEC Exports	Consumed Domestically	Consumed in Rest of EEC	Output Consumed in EEC
Benelux	19,200	5,328	2,624	13,872	2,704	16,576
France	204,000	53,092	50,397	150,908	2,695	153,603
Germany	312,000	110,067	95,223	201,933	14,844	216,777
Italy	25,200	6,713	6,713	18,487	192	18,679
						405,635
1963:						
Wool Fabrics (t)						
Benelux	44,280	9,701	1,988	34,579	7,713	42,293
France	82,870	6,482	2,700	76,388	3,782	80,170
Germany	60,960	3,270	1,850	57,690	1,420	59,110
Italy	85,920	48,154	25,447	37,666	22,707	60,373
						241,946
Cotton Fabrics (t)						
Benelux	288,400	57,680	25,003	230,720	32,677	263,397
France	226,800	40,957	28,087	185,743	12,870	198,613
Germany	260,400	27,068	19,455	233,332	7,613	240,945
Italy	138,000	7,130	5,939	130,870	1,191	132,061
						835,016

Table 19, Continued

1963:	(1)	(2)	(3)	(4)	(5)	
			Non-	((1)-(2))	((2)-(3))	((4)+(5))
Rayon/Acetate Yarn (t)	Total Output	Total Exports	EEC Exports	Consumed Domestically	Consumed in Rest of EEC	Output Consumed in EEC
Benelux	58, 320	42, 502	19, 855	15, 818	22, 547	38, 365
France	58, 560	26, 450	18, 753	32, 110	7, 697	39, 807
Germany	78, 600	40, 898	28, 654	37, 602	12, 244	49, 846
Italy	88, 920	50, 451	37, 577	38, 469	12, 874	51, 343
						179, 361
Agricultural Tractors (#)						
Benelux	3, 500	875	54	2, 525	821	3, 345
France	103, 680	16, 180	7, 518	87, 500	8, 662	96, 162
Germany	162, 720	44, 063	15, 885	118, 657	28, 178	146, 835
Italy	53, 760	17, 951	10, 826	35, 809	7, 125	42, 934
						289, 276
Automobiles (#)						
Benelux	300, 000	162, 555	35, 820	137, 445	126, 735	264, 180
France	1, 453, 200	526, 986	238, 975	926, 214	288, 011	1, 214, 225
Germany	2, 185, 200	1, 280, 191	841, 672	905, 009	438, 519	1, 343, 528
Italy	1, 105, 200	251, 946	108, 059	853, 254	143, 887	997, 141
						3, 817, 074

(continued)

Table 19, Continued

1963: Commercial Vehicles (#)	(1) Total Output	(2) Total Exports	(3) Non-EEC Exports	(4) ((1)-(2)) Consumed Domestically	(5) ((2)-(3)) Consumed in Rest of EEC	((4)+(5)) Output Consumed in EEC
Benelux	30,000	11,577	2,038	18,323	9,539	27,862
France	253,200	46,536	30,644	206,564	15,892	222,456
Germany	476,400	118,484	74,573	357,916	43,911	401,827
Italy	75,600	19,708	11,707	55,892	8,001	63,893
						716,038

Newsprint		Output	World Exports	Domestic Use	EEC Exports	EEC	Use %
1958	Belg.-Lux.	89,000	40,167	48,833	30,926	797,759	7.6
	France	422,000	4,024	417,976	20	417,996	39.7
	Germany	244,000	626	243,374	625	243,999	23.2
	Italy	187,000	593	186,407	484	186,891	17.7
	Netherlands	126,000	40,794	85,206	39,969	125,175	11.9
1963	Belg.-Lux.	99,000	38,843	60,157	35,661	95,818	7.5
	France	435,000	6,170	428,830	5,230	434,060	33.9
	Germany	229,000	3,329	225,671	3,309	228,980	17.9
	Italy	371,000	2,330	368,570	199	368,869	28.8
	Netherlands	152,000	45,304	106,696	45,293	151,989	11.9

Table 19, Continued

Beer		Output	World Exports	Domestic Use	EEC Exports	EEC	Use
							%
1958	Belg.-Lux.	10,148	137	10,011	115	10,126	14.4
	France	17,573	126	17,447	19	14,766	21.0
	Germany	42,244	1,249	40,995	450	41,445	59.0
	Italy	1,658	14	1,644	0	1,644	2.3
	Netherlands	2,941	723	2,218	0	2,218	3.2
1963	Belg.-Lux.	11,400	497	10,903	486	11,389	11.4
	France	17,900	374	17,526	93	17,619	17.6
	Germany	64,300	874	63,426	355	63,781	63.6
	Italy	3,700	16	3,684	0	3,684	3.7
	Netherlands	4,400	791	3,609	257	3,866	3.9
Sugar							
1958	Belg.-Lux.	471,000	103,582	353,418	9,719	363,137	7.5
	France	1,565,000	471,670	1,093,330	9,114	1,102,444	22.7
	Germany	1,763,000	12,965	1,750,205	28	1,750,230	36.1
	Italy	1,118,000	15,823	1,102,177	7	1,102,184	22.7
	Netherlands	577,000	47,003	529,997	6,858	536,855	11.1
1963	Belg.-Lux.	351,000	66,900	284,100	12,947	297,047	7.2
	France	1,650,000	838,907	811,993	226,764	1,038,757	25.0
	Germany	1,390,000	4,010	1,385,990	2,609	1,388,599	33.5
	Italy	998,000	10,033	987,967	9,998	997,965	24.1
	Netherlands	437,000	15,568	421,332	4,428	425,860	10.3

BIBLIOGRAPHY

BIBLIOGRAPHY

Bachmann, Hans. "Die Vereinbarungen von Handelsumlenkungen in einer Freihandelszone," Aussenwirtschaft (March-June, 1958).

Balassa, Bela. The Theory of Economic Integration. Homewood, Ill.: Richard D. Irwin, 1962.

Beckerman, W. "Distance and the Pattern of Intra-European Trade," Review of Economics and Statistics (February, 1956).

Bertrand, R. "Comparison du Niveau des Tarifs duaniers des Pays du Marché Commun." Paris: Institut de Science Economique Appliqué, 1958.

Binswanger, Hans-Christoph. "Der Zollschutz in den Laendern der europaeischen Wirtschaftsgemeinschaft und in der Schweiz," in Die europaeische Wirtschaftsgemeinschaft im Banne des Gemeinsamen Marktes. Zurich: Polygraphischer Verlag, 1959.

Committee for Economic Development. European Tariffs and Trade. New York: CED, 1962.

Cosciani, C. "Problèmes Fiscaux de la Communauté Economique Européenne," Public Finance, VIII, No. 1 (March, 1958).

Dell, Sidney. Trade Blocs and Common Markets. New York: Alfred A. Knopf, 1963.

Deniau, Jean-François. The Common Market. New York: Praeger, 1960.

Economist Intelligence Unit. "Tariffs on a Cross-Section of 28 Import Categories," in Britain and Europe. London: EIU, 1957.

EEC Commission. Reports on the Execution of the Treaty (Brussels), various issues, 1958-63.

Erdmann, Paul, and Rogge, Peter. Die europaeische Wirtschaftsgemeinschaft und die Drittlaender. Basel: Kyklos-Verlag, 1960.

European Communities, Statistical Office. Allgemeines Statistisches Bulletin. Luxembourg: European Communities, various issues, 1953-65 inclusive.

___, Statistical Office. Analytische Uebersichten: Ausfuhr. Luxembourg: European Communities, various issues, 1953-65 inclusive.

___, Statistical Office. Analytische Uebersichten: Einfuhr. Luxembourg: European Communities, various issues, 1953-65 inclusive.

___, Statistical Office. Industriestatistik. Luxembourg: European Communities, various issues, 1953-65 inclusive.

___, Statistical Office. "Méthodes de Prévision du développement économique à long-terme," Informations Statistiques. (November-December, 1960.)

Frank, Isaiah. The European Common Market. New York: Praeger, 1961.

Gehrels, Franz. "Customs Unions from a Single-Country Viewpoint," Review of Economic Studies (1956-57).

Gehrels, Franz, and Johnston, Bruce F. "The Economic Gains of European Integration," Journal of Political Economy (August, 1955).

Groeben, Hans von der, and Boeckh, H. von. Kommentar zum EWG-Vertrag. Baden-Baden: August Lutzeyer, 1958.

Haberler, Gottfried. A Survey of International Trade Theory. Princeton: International Finance Section, Department of Economics, Princeton University, 1961.

High Authority, European Coal and Steel Community. Report on the Problems Posed by the Turnover Tax to the Common Market. Luxembourg: High Authority, ECSC, 1953.

Hinshaw, Randall. The European Community and American Trade. New York: Praeger, 1964.

Hochbaum, M. Das Diskriminierungs - und Subventions - verbot in der EGKS und EWG. Baden-Baden: August Lutzeyer, 1962.

Horn, J. van. "Das Problem der Harmonisierung der Steuern innerhalb der EWG," Deutsches Verwaltungsblatt, 1961.

Interim Committee for the Common Market and EURATOM. Treaty Establishing the European Atomic Energy Community (EURATOM) and the Common Market, and connected documents. Brussels: Interim Committee, 1957.

International Monetary Fund. International Financial Statistics. Washington, D.C.: IMF, various issues, 1953-65 inclusive.

Jensen, Finn B., and Walter, Ingo. The Common Market: Economic Integration in Europe. Philadelphia: J.B. Lippincott Company, 1965.

Johnson, Harry G. "The European Common Market: Risk or Opportunity?" Weltwirtschaftliches Archiv, No. 2 (1957).

Junckersdorff, H.K. (ed.). International Manual on the European Community. St. Louis: St. Louis University Press, 1963.

Kerrmann, K. Europas Handelswirtschaftliche Einheit von Morgen. Baden-Baden: August Lutzeyer, 1960.

Kindleberger, Charles P. International Economics. Homewood, Ill.: Richard D. Irwin, 1963.

Kitzinger, Uwe. The Politics and Economics of European Integration. New York: Praeger, 1964.

Korbonski, Andrzej. "Comecon," International Conciliation (September, 1964).

Kravis, Irving B., Lipsey, Robert E., and Bourque, Philip J. Measuring International Price Competitiveness, a Preliminary Report. National Bureau of Economic Research, Occasional Paper, No. 94. New York, 1965.

Kreinin, M. E. "On the 'Trade-Diversion' Effect of Trade Preference Areas," Journal of Political Economy (August, 1959).

Krenzel, R. "Die wirtschaftlichen Integrationsbestrebungen und Integrationshindernisse im Ostblock," in Ostblock, EWG und Entwicklungslaender. Edited by E. Boettcher. Stuttgart: W. Kohlhammer, 1963.

Lamfalussy, Alexander. "Europe's Progress: Due to Common Market?" in The Common Market, Progress and Controversy. Edited by L. B. Krause. Englewood Cliffs, N.J.: Prentice-Hall, 1964.

___. The United Kingdom and the Six. Homewood, Ill.: Richard D. Irwin, 1963.

Linder, Staffan B. An Essay on Trade and Transformation. Stockholm: Almquist and Wicksell, 1961.

Lipsey, R. G. "The Theory of Customs Unions: A General Survey," Economic Journal (September, 1960).

Lister, Louis. Europe's Coal and Steel Community. New York: Twentieth Century Fund, 1960.

Mankower, H., and Morton, G. "A Contribution to the Theory of Customs Unions," Economic Journal (March, 1953).

Marcey, G. "How Far Can Foreign Trade and Customs Agreements Confer Upon Small Nations the Advantages of Large Nations?" in Economic Consequences of the Size of Nations. Edited by E. A. G. Robinson. London: Macmillan, 1960.

Mayne, Richard. The Community of Europe. New York: Norton, 1962.

Meade, James E. Problems of Economic Union. Chicago: University of Chicago Press, 1953.

___. The Theory of Customs Unions. Amsterdam: North Holland Publishing Company, 1955.

___. Trade and Welfare. London: Oxford University Press, 1955.

Megow, Heinrich. Steuern und Zoelle im Gemeinsamen Markt. Baden-Baden: August Lutzeyer, 1962.

Meyer, F.V. "Complementarity and the Lowering of Tariffs," American Economic Review (June, 1956).

Organization for Economic Cooperation and Development. Foreign Trade Statistics. Paris: OEEC/OECD, various issues, 1953-65.

___. General Statistics. Paris: OEEC/OECD, various issues, 1953-66.

___. International Trade, 1961. Paris: OECD, 1962.

Perroux, François. L'intégration Européenne. Paris: Sirey, 1958.

Political and Economic Planning. Trade Diversion in Europe. London: PEP, 1960.

Pryor, F. L. The Communist Foreign Trade System. Cambridge: MIT Press, 1963.

Roepke, Wilhelm. "Gemeinsamer Markt und Freihandelszone," Ordo (July, 1958).

Sainte Lorette, L. de. Le Marché Commun. Paris: Colin, 1960.

Salant, Walter S. et al. The United States Balance of Payments in 1968. Washington, D.C.: The Brookings Institution, 1963.

Sannwald, Rolf, and Stohler, Jacques. Economic Integration. Princeton: Princeton University Press, 1959.

Schmoelders, Guenther. Steuerliche Wettbewerbsverzerrungen beim Grenzueberschreitenden Warenverkehr im Gemeinsamen Markt. Cologne: Carl Heymanns Verlag, 1962.

Scitovsky, Tibor. Economic Theory and Western European Integration. Stanford: Stanford University Press, 1958.

___. "A Reconsideration of the Theory of Tariffs," in Readings in the Theory of International Trade. American Economic Association. Homewood, Ill.: Richard D. Irwin, 1949.

Der Spiegel. "Die deutschen Bauern wehren sich" (November 15, 1964).

___. "Waehrung: Inflation via Brussel" (July 1, 1964).

Thorbecke, Erik. The Tendency Toward Regionalization in International Trade. The Hague: Martinus Nijhoff, 1960.

Tinbergen, Jan. "Customs Unions: Influence of Their Size and Their Effect," Zeitschrift fuer die gesamte Staatswissenschaft, No. 4 (1957).

___. International Economic Integration. 2nd ed. Amsterdam: Elsevier, 1965.

___. Selected Papers. Amsterdam: North Holland Publishing Company, 1959.

___. Shaping the World Economy. New York: Twentieth Century Fund, 1962.

Topping, Francis K. "Comparative Tariffs and Trade." Supplementary Paper No. 14. New York: Committee for Economic Development, 1963.

United Nations, Economic Commission for Europe. Economic Survey of Europe. Geneva: U.N., 1956, 1960, 1963.

United Nations, Secretariat, Statistical Office. Monthly

Bulletin of Statistics. New York: U.N., various issues, 1953-65 inclusive.

___. Statistical Papers, Series D. Commodity Trade Statistics. New York: U.N., various issues, 1953-65 inclusive.

___. Statistical Papers, Series T. Direction of International Trade. New York: U.N., various issues, 1953-65 inclusive.

___. Statistical Yearbook. New York: U.N., various issues, 1953-65 inclusive.

___. Yearbook of National Accounts Statistics. New York: U.N., various issues, 1953-65 inclusive.

Vanek, Jaroslav. General Equilibrium of International Discrimination. Cambridge: Harvard University Press, 1965.

___. International Trade: Theory and Economic Policy. Homewood, Ill.: Richard D. Irwin, 1962.

Vedel, G. "Les Aspects fiscaux du Marché Commun," Bulletin for Industrial Fiscal Documentation (Amsterdam), No. 12 (1960).

Verdoorn, Pieter Jan. "A Customs Union for Western Europe - Advantages and Feasibility," World Politics (July, 1954).

___. "The Intra-Bloc Trade of the Benelux," in Economic Consequences of the Size of Nations. Edited by E. A. G. Robinson. London: Macmillan, 1960.

___, and Schlocten, F. J. M. Meyer zu. "Trade Diversion and Trade Creation in the Common Market," Central Planning Bureau Reprint Series, No. 93 (The Hague, 1965).

Viner, Jacob. The Customs Union Issue. New York: Carnegie Endowment for International Peace, 1950.

Wagenheim, J. V. "Der Einfluss der Steuern auf die

Wettbewerbslage im gemeinsamen Stahlmarkt," Der Volkswirt (supplement), No. 46 (November 17, 1961).

Wemsfelder, J. "Verhindern Unterschiede in der Wirtschaftspolitik der Europaeischen Laender den Abbau der Handelsschranken?" in M. Byé, et. al., Europas Wirtschaftseinheit von Morgen. Baden-Baden: August Lutzeyer, 1960.

Wionczek, Miguel S. "Latin American Free Trade Association," International Conciliation (January, 1965).

ABOUT THE AUTHOR

Ingo Walter is Assistant Professor of Economics at the University of Missouri at St. Louis. He is joint author of The Common Market: Economic Integration in Europe, published in 1965, and joint editor of International Economic Relations, published in 1966. Professor Walter has also contributed to a study on U.S. exports to Latin America. Other publications include a monograph on the Central American Common Market and a forthcoming textbook on international economic theory. Dr. Walter recently has done extensive research in Western Europe, focusing on regional planning programs that have been instituted in several European countries.

Professor Walter received his A. B. and M. S. degrees in economics from Lehigh University and his Ph.D. from New York University, where he held a Ford Foundation Doctoral Fellowship in Economic Growth.